D1824680

THE PHONEY CLUB
Cleveland Club System

by

David Marsh-Smith

DORRANCE PUBLISHING CO., INC.
PITTSBURGH, PENNSYLVANIA 15222

FOR BILL

Table of Contents

Introduction

Many players use a "Phoney Club" or artificial club bid because they feel uncomfortable with systems which do not distinguish between four-card and longer suits in the early bidding. Devotees of "standard" systems such as Acol or Goren often look down their noses at such players. It is the purpose of this book to describe an accurate bidding system based on the Phoney Club and to illustrate its advantages over Acol. While it may at first sight seem more complicated, as an Acol teacher I can assure you that this is an illusion.

The basic problem with Acol and with other standard systems is that the opening bid of one of a suit, which starts most auctions, is singularly uninformative. It might indicate a weak but shapely hand of some 10 high card points, or a hand with no five-card suit up to 19 points, or even a strong suited hand not qualifying for a two bid. The suit could be of four to seven cards, or even three of a minor. The unlimited nature of the opening bid necessitates the use of an artificial weak 1NT response. This bid in turn gives little or no indication of hand shape and causes any final NT contract to be played by the wrong hand. Of course, standard players can cope with most other situations if there is no intervening bid. However, when playing standard systems with a strong NT opener, what do you say when your right-hand opponent bids 2♦ over his partner's vulnerable 1♥ opener when holding:

    ♠ Qx   ♥ xxx   ♦ Jxxx   ♣ Axxx ?

Your partner could have a hand like:

    a) ♠ Kxxx   b) ♠ Axx   c) ♠ Axx
       ♥ Axxx   ♥ KJxxxx   ♥ AKQxx
       ♦ Ax   ♦ x   ♦ Kx
       ♣ Qxx   ♣ Qxx   ♣ Kxx

Experts disagree about which suit partner should open with hands like a), but in any case it is best to pass. If he has a hand like b) or c) it is better to bid. With no intervening bid, the standard pair would end in 1NT with a), 2♥ with b) and a game contract with c). It is the lack of information about the length of the heart suit which makes the intervening bid so difficult to handle.

In the Cleveland Club system, only hand b) would open 1♥. With no opposition bidding, hand a) would play in 1♥ after an opening 1♣ bid.

It is not feasible to graft a Phoney Club bid on to another system: This can cause problems. What follows is a consistent club system described in terms of an accurate method of hand valuation. This system aims to keep the number of artificial bids and complications to the minimum necessary.

The Phoney Club has been suppressed for too long. The time has come for glasnost and perestroika.

PART ONE: MAKING A SYSTEM

CHAPTER ONE:
FUNDAMENTALS

The main object of a system of bidding in Contract Bridge is to determine whether a game can probably be made. The great majority of games are made either in No Trumps or in a major suit. Even when a game could be made in 5♦ or 5♣, it is often easier to make 3NT, and there is also a better chance of over tricks. On the other hand, if there is an adequate number of trumps, it is usually easier to make 4♠ or 4♥ than 3NT.

It follows that the main objective can be restated as determining whether the partnership has enough strength for a game try and enough spades or hearts to make the try in a major suit.

Hand Valuation

The value of a hand is made up of two parts, high card strength and distribution. In valuing, we are trying to predict how many tricks will result from these strengths. In the case of high cards, the various methods used during the past fifty or so years of Contract Bridge have given way to an almost universal acceptance of one. This is the point count method of Ace 4, King 3, Queen 2, and Jack 1. This is the one we will use, although it is in some ways inferior to 7,5,3,1 for slam bidding.

In predicting the trick-taking value of a hand, one assumes that there will be three rounds of each suit, with the thirteenth trick going to the side which has control. The total number of points is 40 and the average number in a hand is 10. It follows that the expected trick-taking value of 10 points is three. Roughly speaking we can expect the Ace, King, and Queen to take tricks, the average high card winner being the King. I use the term "winner" to represent expected trick-taking value. We can use the general formula:

$$\text{High Card Winners} = \frac{\text{Points -1}}{3}$$

$$W = \frac{P-1}{3}$$

We now have our high card values in a form which can be directly added to distribution values to give the total expectation of tricks. However, in normal No Trump hands it is not necessary to go beyond points.

In determining distributional winners, one again assumes there will be three rounds of each suit. If we have a doubleton, we can ruff the third round of the suit, and with a singleton we can limit our losses to one. In practice, this may be done by the use of long cards in a side suit or by ruffing. Our distributional winners are the sum of the number of cards under three in each of the side suits.

For example, in:

♠ AKxxxx   ♥ Ax   ♦ x   ♣ Qxxx

Where x represents a card below a Jack, the total points are 13 and the distributional winners 3 (1 in hearts and 2 in diamonds). Total winners are 4 from the high cards and 3 from distribution, making 7.

Two more examples:

	Points	Distributional Winners	Total Winners
♠ KJxx ♥ KJx ♦ KJx ♣ KJx	16	0	5
♠ AJxxx ♥ AJxxx ♦ xx ♣ x	10	3	6

We can refine the method by considering unguarded honours. A single honour is associated with two distributional winners because it is a singleton, but it obviously has less value as a high card. We deduct one point when considering its contribution to winners.

♠ A   ♥ KQJxxx ♦ KJx   ♣ xxx   (14) 13   2   6

In this example, the Ace single counts only three for determining winners.

All the above examples show winners as a whole number. However, if P-1 is not divisible by 3, we can have a fraction in the answer. 1/3W is a 33 percent chance of a trick and 2/3W is a 67 percent chance. We will use the notation ·1 for 1/3 and ·2 for 2/3 of a winner in the examples. ·1 represents 1 extra high card point and ·2 represents 2 extra high card points, 3 points being a winner. When adding, ·1 + ·2 = 1.

This method of counting winners allows full value for distribution. Methods allowing one "point" for a doubleton and two "points" for a singleton only allow 1/3 of the potential value. To take an extreme example which illustrates this, consider a hand consisting of one suit only:

♠ AKQJ1098765432	10 points	3 winners
♥ -		3 distributional winners
♦ -		3 " "
♣ -		3 " "
		12 total winners

Such a hand, having control, will also take the thirteenth trick. Compare the rival valuation of 3 "points" for each of the voids which gives a total for "points" of 19, well below the accepted level for a game bid. Actually, Acol rules would give the "points" for suit length and allow "points" for side suit shortages only for the responding hand.

I consider it unsound to call distributional values points: It can lead to confusion and to adding "oranges and apples." It is also a symptom of undervaluing distribution compared with high cards. To illustrate this, I ask my students the minimum number of points needed for a grand slam assuming favourable distribution of opposing cards. The answer is 5; e.g., 7♠:

♠ Axxxx	♠ Jxxxxx
♥ -	♥ xxx
♦ -	♦ xxxx
♣ xxxxxxxx	♣ -

To return to the main objective of bidding, one must decide whether and in what denomination a game should be bid. The calculations in the appendix show that, although vulnerability increases the stakes, it does not alter the odds affecting the decision. One should bid game if there is almost a 50 percent chance of making it. Similarly with slams, vulnerability does not affect the decision. Small slams should be bid with a 50 percent or better chance and grand slams with a 67 percent chance.

No Trump Game

When there are no trumps, the main factor to be considered is high card values. It is generally accepted, as shown in the appendix, that 25 points in two hands is sufficient for bidding 3NT. Since we obviously should not risk passing with the possibility of 25 points, we must not pass a thirteen-point hand. With 12 points each, however, there is not an adequate chance of game in NT. This determines that the minimum number of points for a bid with a No Trump sort of hand should be 13.

Games with a Trump Suit

We have already considered that a minor suit game is unlikely to be the best try when we can make 3NT. Therefore we base our calculation on a major suit game of ten tricks.

When considering total winners, i.e., high card winners plus distributional winners in both hands of a partnership, there is another factor to be borne in mind. This is the possibility of duplication of values between the two hands. For example, one partner may hold the King of a suit where the other partner has a singleton. It is one of the purposes of bidding to find out how likely this duplication is — in other words, the likelihood of a fit.

At the level of about ten tricks, experience shows that duplication of values is likely to cost one trick. On the other hand, if we have an adequate number of trumps, we expect to have control of the hand. That is, we expect to make the "thirteenth trick" and can add one for this. We can therefore ignore both duplication and the control trick until the process of bidding shows otherwise.

Our trick expectation when we have adequate trumps is therefore simply $W1 + W2$, where these represent the total winners in each hand of the partnership. If we do not have an adequate number of trumps, and especially if partner's suit is opposite a shortage in our hand and vice versa, the method of adding winners does not apply.

We wish to bid game if we have a near-50 percent or better chance of making it, i.e., a trick expectation of not less than $9 \cdot 2$ (i.e., $9\,{}^2/_3$); that is, if $W1 + W2 = 9 \cdot 2$ or more. This shows that we must normally bid if we have 5 winners or better in a hand likely to lead to a suit contract.

Trump Control

We obviously do not wish to play in a suit contract unless we have, with our partner, a majority of trumps. Holding seven, we have a slight majority over our opponents who have six. In this case, however, the chances of one opponent's holding four or more are rather high — about 2 out of 3. The most likely division of six cards is four and two. This means that seven cards in the trump suit cannot be expected to be a working majority.

The situation is radically different when we hold eight trumps compared with the opponents' five. In this case the most probable division of the five is three and two, the odds in favour being 2 out of 3. It follows that a combined eight cards in the trump suit is normally a working majority.

One of the prime objectives in bidding is to find out if we and our partner hold eight cards of a major suit.

Types of Hands

For the purpose of bidding, I divide hands between those that have one or more five-card suits "suited hands" and those whose longest suit is four cards. If we have a five-card suit, it is quite likely that our partner will have three or more cards; that is, that we hold at least eight, the working majority. If our suit is only four cards, there is only about 1 chance in 3 that our partner holds four or more. This means that suited hands expect to play with a trump suit, while the others are more likely to play in No Trumps. Therefore we value suited hands by winners, whereas with the No Trumps type there is no need to go beyond points unless and until a four-four fit is found.

Limit Bids

Any uncontested sequence of bids proceeds until one partner has defined his hand accurately enough for the other partner to determine the final contract. A bid which defines the hand between agreed close limits is called a limit bid. It is a bid which gives the maximum useful information about the hand. It took some years after Contract Bridge was invented for this concept to be appreciated fully. The best systems are those which have the most frequently occurring limit bids. Conversely, a system which has many frequently used unlimited bids can be expected to be a poor one. For many years, those systems which limit the opening bid of one of a suit have had a tremendous advantage, starting with the all-conquering Austrian system in the Thirties. If all opening bids can be relatively closely limited, so much the better.

CHAPTER TWO:
TACTICAL CONSIDERATIONS

Three themes will influence our choice under the heading of tactics. These are: the advantage of being the first bidder, the frequency of the use of bids, and the advantage of having the right hand as declarer.

In order to avoid losing too many rounds of bidding, we must restrict normal opening bids to the one or two level. There are just ten of these. We want to open the bidding with suited hands as often as possible. This is most conveniently arranged by having a light opening bid of one of a suit subject to a minimum of 5 winners. Since we want this to be a limit bid, we must use the two-level suit bids for hands of intermediate strength and abandon thoughts of a weak two bid, or a very strong two.

This concept also fits in with the economic use of our ten possible bids. Those systems which use all two bids for strong hands are sacrificing five bids for hands which are rare. Similarly, the weak two-bids based on six-card suits are rather infrequent.

The third of our tactical considerations, the choice of the correct hand as declarer, shows that No Trump bids should not be used on weak hands. We want the lead to come up to a strong hand and it is often an advantage for the strong hand to be hidden.

Constructing the System

We choose limit opening bids for both suited and non-suited hands as follows:

Non-suited or No Trump Seeking Hands

These are hands with 4,3,3,3, and 4,4,3,2 distribution; we must also accommodate 4,4,4,1. With normal lazy shuffling they occur in total in a little under half the cases. The most frequent distribution of all is 4,4,3,2. The 4,4,4,1 distribution, which only happens in 3 percent of hands, is a special case and is always opened ♣1 or ♣2, if strong enough to open.

13 - 15 points	open 1♣
16 - 19 points	open 1NT
20 - 22 points	open 2NT
23 or more points	open 2♣

Suited Hands

The most frequent distributions are 5,5,3,2; 5,4,3,1; 5,4,2,2; 6,3,2,2; 6,3,3,1; and 5,5,2,1.

5 - 6·2 winners	open 1 suit
7 - 8·1 winners	open 2♠, 2♥, 2♦, or 1♣
8·2 or more winners	open 2♣

In neither series are there any gaps, the range of strength for each bid touching the next.

The bid 1♣ most commonly applies to the weak No Trump type of hand, and is assumed by partner to mean this until a contrary indication is given. Because of the low expectation of game in a minor suit, the club suit is used for a number of artificial bids. However, we do not need to use the diamond suit so often in this way, and it is better left to its natural use.

Responses

Bearing in mind the requirements for the various limit opening bids, it is easy to construct a table of responses. When there is no chance of game even when the opener is at the maximum, the responder should pass. If the likely outcome is No Trumps, the response is based on a count of points; otherwise, on a count of winners.

As a principle, only a five-card or longer suit may be shown as a first response to the non-suit opening bids (1♣ or 1 or 2 NT). In response to a long suit opening bid, a higher-ranking four-card suit may be bid at the minimum level. This obviously can only be a major suit. First responses of lower ranking suits are reserved for five-card or longer suits.

In all cases, four-card suits may be shown subsequently if the circumstances allow.

Responding Points

6 - 8 points	minimum response to a strong opener (1NT, 2♠, 2♥, 2♦)
9 - 11 points	minimum positive response to a weak opener (1♠, 1♥, 1♦, or 1♣)
12 or more points	forcing response to a weak opener

Responding Winners (approximate)

2 - 2·2 winners	minimum response to a strong opener
3 - 3·2 winners	minimum response to a weak opener

There follows a more detailed description of the system. It should be remembered that the opening bid determines the type of bidding sequences which follow it. After an opening of 1♠, ♥, or ♦, bidding is natural. 1♣ starts a special series, as does a bid of 2 of a suit, while after 1 or 2NT bidding is mainly natural apart from a single artificial convention.

In the examples, points and winners are shown thus 13/6, as in:

	♠ AKQxxx
13/6	♥ Axx
	♦ xxx
	♣ x

X is used for any card below a Jack for the sake of simplicity. However, intermediate cards — tens and nines — may influence bidding decisions in borderline cases.

Each hand maintains its original valuation, but if there is no trump agreement the winners cannot be added together. For example, if partner opens 1♥, we still count 3 winners and reply 1♠ with:

♠ Axxxx   ♥ xx   ♦ Kxx   ♣ xxx   7/3

in the hope that he has spade support. Even if we play in hearts, the distributional value of the spade suit length may be of use.

In the examples, the following slam conventions are used:

(i) Blackwood 4NT for Aces and Kings when a trump suit has been agreed.

(ii) 5NT Grand Slam Force when not preceded by the Blackwood 4NT for locating the top three trumps.

(iii) Cue bids of Aces or voids at the four level when the trump suit is agreed.

There may be exceptions when the bidding has started with 2 of a major.

33 points are regarded as adequate for bidding a small slam in NT and 37 points for a grand slam.

PART TWO:
THE SYSTEM

CHAPTER THREE:
LIMITED OPENING BIDS WITH
SUITED HANDS 1♠, 1♥, AND 1♦

Requirements for Opening Bids

These bids are limit bids on hands with one or more five-card or longer suits, the range of strength being 5 - 6·2 winners.

Handling the club suit will be covered in the next chapter.

One Spade, One Heart

The minimum points requirement is normally 10, and this would need at least 2 distributional winners associated with either a two-suiter or a six-card suit. The maximum number of points is 17.

Minimum hands have either 5,3,3,2 distribution with 13 - 15 points or are more unbalanced with 10-12 points. Bid 1♠ on:

	♠ AQxxx			♠ AQxxxx			♠ KQxxx
13/5	♥ KQx		10/5	♥ Axx		10/5	♥ AJxx
	♦ Qxx			♦ xx			♦ xxx
	♣ xx			♣ xx			♣ x

Maximum hands have either 13 - 15 points and two distributional winners or 5,3,3,2 with 16 or 17 points. Bid 1♠ on:

	♠ KJxxx			♠ AKJxx
14/6·1	♥ AQxx		17/6·1	♥ AJx
	♦ Ax			♦ Axx
	♣ xx			♣ xx

One Diamond

The requirements for 1♦ are similar to those for one of a major except that the range of strength is narrowed slightly. 5,3,3,2 hands of 16 or 17 points open 1NT rather than 1♦, while a minimum point or distributional hand must have either a six-card suit or subsidiary (four-card) major.

Choice of Suits When Holding Two of Five Cards or Longer

Normally, choose the longer suit or the higher ranking of equal-length suits. If, however, the suits are six-card diamonds and a five-card major, preference should be given to the major. See the next chapter for a further exception involving the club suit.

Requirements for Responses

Responses to 1♠, 1♥, and 1♦

As shown above, the minimum opening hand is of similar strength to English and American standard systems, but the maximum is curtailed in a similar fashion to the Precision Club and Austrian Systems. This affects the responses and removes the need to bid poor hands in case your partner is strong. In particular, there is no need for the artificial weak No Trump response, with its twin drawbacks of a possible penalty double when the opener is weak and playing the hand the wrong way around in Three No Trumps when he is strong.

1. Direct Suit Raises

These are all limit bids made with trump support and are based on a count of winners assuming the opener has five.

Raise to two with 3 - 3·2 winners — also 2·2 winners when holding four or more of partner's suit.

Raise to three with 4 - 4·1 winners and a fairly balanced hand.

Raise a major suit to four with more than 4 winners and an unbalanced hand.

E.g., raise 1♥ to two with:

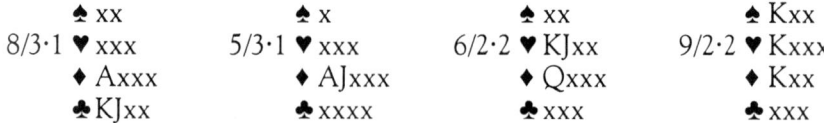

	♠ xx		♠ x		♠ xx		♠ Kxx
8/3·1	♥ xxx	5/3·1	♥ xxx	6/2·2	♥ KJxx	9/2·2	♥ Kxxx
	♦ Axxx		♦ AJxxx		♦ Qxxx		♦ Kxx
	♣ KJxx		♣ xxxx		♣ xxx		♣ xxx

14

Raise to three with:		Raise to four with:	
♠ x	♠ Ax	♠ x	♠ x
8/4·1 ♥ Jxx	11/4·1 ♥ Jxxx	5/4·1 ♥ Jxxxx	8/5·1 ♥ AQxx
♦ Axxxx	♦ Kxx	♦ Axxxx	♦ Qxxxxx
♣ Kxxx	♣ Kxxx	♣ xx	♣ xx

Direct suit raises combine the possibility of advancing to game with the maximum obstruction to the opponent's bidding. However, over 1♦, an alternative response should be chosen if the hand has enough points for a NT game to be a possibility, or if it has a major suit.

2. Responses in No Trumps

a) 1NT is a limit response showing 9 - 11 points and either a non-suit hand or 5,3,3,2 with the five-card suit a minor. Usually, two cards of partner's suit will be held.

E.g., over 1♥ bid 1NT with:

	♠ Kxx	♠ Kxx	♠ Kxx
10 points	♥ xx	9/2·2 ♥ xxx	9/3·2 ♥ xx
(4 winners)	♦ Axxx	♦ Axx	♦ Axxxx
	♣ QJxx	♣ Qxxx	♣ Qxx

but with ♠ KJxx ♥ xx ♦ KQxx ♣ xxx 9/3·2 bid 1♠. It may be more important to find a spade fit than to commit the partnership to No Trumps.

b) 2NT. This response, which is unlimited and forcing to game, is made on balanced hands (non-suited) of at least 12 points. Either high cards in the other suits or trump support should be held.

Over 1♥ Bid 2NT with:

♠ KJxx	♠ KJx	♠ AKxx	♠ Kxxx
13/5 ♥ xx	13/4 ♥ xxx	17/6·1 ♥ xx	15/5·2 ♥ KJxx
♦ KQxx	♦ KQxx	♦ AKxx	♦ Ax
♣ Axx	♣ Axx	♣ Kxx	♣ Axx

The last two examples are not ideal for a jump take-out in a suit, while the last is too strong for a jump suit raise.

This bid requires the opener to bid his second suit or to bid 3NT if he has 5,3,3,2 distribution.

c) The 3NT response is a limit bid showing 4,3,3,3 distribution with 15 or 16 points. It is a mild slam suggestion.

3. Suit Responses

Responses at the one level (major suits) can be made with four-card suits but require at least 3 winners. Being unlimited, they are forcing for one round.

Non-jump suit responses at the two level require five-card suits and at least 9 points or a longer suit with about 4 or more winners. They are also forcing for one round.

Jump take-outs are made on strong hands with either trump support (about 6 or more winners), a good suit, or general strength with a five-card suit.

E.g.,

Minimum responses over 1♥:

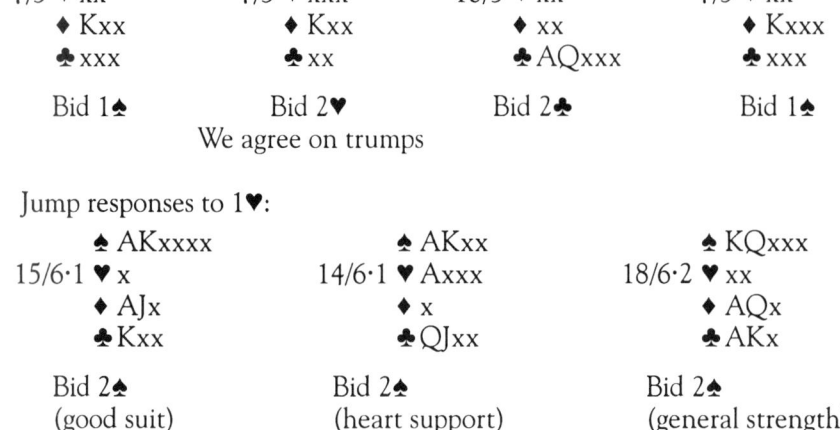

♠ Axxxx	But ♠ Axxxx	♠ Axxx	♠ Axxx
7/3 ♥ xx	7/3 ♥ xxx	10/5 ♥ xx	7/3 ♥ xx
♦ Kxx	♦ Kxx	♦ xx	♦ Kxxx
♣ xxx	♣ xx	♣ AQxxx	♣ xxx
Bid 1♠	Bid 2♥	Bid 2♣	Bid 1♠
	We agree on trumps		

Jump responses to 1♥:

♠ AKxxxx	♠ AKxx	♠ KQxxx
15/6·1 ♥ x	14/6·1 ♥ Axxx	18/6·2 ♥ xx
♦ AJx	♦ x	♦ AQx
♣ Kxx	♣ QJxx	♣ AKx
Bid 2♠	Bid 2♠	Bid 2♠
(good suit)	(heart support)	(general strength)

♠ KQxxx	♠ KQxxx	♠ KQx
15/5·2 ♥ xx	15/5·2 ♥ KQx	15/5·2 ♥ KQxxx
♦ KQx	♦ xx	♦ xx
♣ AJx	♣ AJx	♣ AJx
Only 1♠	Bid 2♠	Choose between
	(heart support)	3♣ and 2NT—
		3♣ preferred

4. The Pass

If there is little hope of game, even if the opener has a maximum, the best course of action is usually to pass. This applies to hands with less than 9 points which do not have trump support or a suitable major suit. Thus the following hands should all be passed opposite 1♥, unless the 8-point hands are loaded with tens and nines.

♠ Kxx	♠ Kxx	♠ Kxxx
8/3·1 ♥ xx	8/2·1 ♥ Kxx	7/2 ♥ Kxx
♦ Kxxxx	♦ xxxx	♦ xxx
♣ Qxx	♣ Qxx	♣ Jxx
lacking points and	lacking winners	lacking winners
trump support		

With the first two hands, we may miss game in 3NT if the opener has 17 points and 5,3,3,2 distribution with a major suit. Other 17-point hands would not open one of a suit.

Rebids by Opener

a) After Direct Suit Raises

As soon as a trump suit is agreed, bidding can proceed on a count of winners. For example, a minimum opener of 5 winners opposite a minimum responder of 3 winners raising to two (5 + 3 = 8) would normally close the bidding. In a non-competitive situation, there is no point in continuing the bidding after partner has supported your major suit, unless there is a hope that total winners could be 9·2 or more.

If the response is a single raise, the opener can therefore continue if he has 6 or more winners. With 6 winners he can make a game try by raising to three, by showing a second suit, or by bidding 2NT. With a maximum of 6·2 winners, he can of course bid the major suit game.

If partner makes a limited raise to three in a major suit, this should normally be converted to game unless a bare minimum is held. Some unbalanced hands may give play for a slam when the second suit may be used to start a slam enquiry.

b) After 1NT Response

The limit response of 1NT can be passed unless the opener's suit is a weak six-carder when it should be repeated at the two level. Other bids indicate extra values.

Examples

When agreement is reached on a trump suit, winners are added as shown. When there is no agreement, the addition is shown in brackets as not applicable. No Trump hands show the addition of points.

13/6	♠ AQxxx ♥ AQJx ♦ xx ♣ xx	11/4·1	♠ Jx ♥ Kxxx ♦ Axx ♣ Kxxx

$$6 + 4\cdot1 = 10\cdot1 \text{ winners}$$

1♠	1NT
2♥	4♥

16/6	♠ Axx ♥ AQJxx ♦ Qxx ♣ Kx	10/4	♠ Kxx ♥ xx ♦ Jxxx ♣ AQxx

$$16 + 10 = 26 \text{ points}$$

1♥	1NT
3NT	

There must be at least 25 points.

c) The 2NT response which is forcing to game may lead to a slam attempt.

13/6	♠ AQxxx ♥ AQJx ♦ xx ♣ xx	16/6	♠ Kxx ♥ Kxxx ♦ AQxx ♣ Ax

$$6 + 6 = 12$$

1♠	2NT
3♥	5♥ (he is not
6♥ (extra	worried about
winner and	controls)
good hearts)	

10/5	♠ AQxxxx ♥ KJx ♦ xx ♣ xx	14/5·1	♠ Jx ♥ Axxx ♦ KQxx ♣ Axx

$$5 + 5\cdot1 = 10\cdot1$$

1♠	2NT
3♠	4♠

The spade rebid shows six cards, so the responder, with his points in the higher honours, chooses the major suit game rather than 3NT.

d) After the limit 3NT response, the opener can pass or rebid his suit to indicate no interest in a slam. Other bids show slam hopes.

	♠ KQxxxx		♠ Axx
14/6·1	♥ KQx	16/5	♥ Axx
	♦ Axx		♦ Kxx
	♣ x		♣ AJxx

$$6·1 + 5 + 1 = 12·1$$

1♠	3NT
4NT (Blackwood)	5♠ (3 Aces)
6♠	

West can add 1 winner for known lack of duplication after the three Aces are shown.

e) Suit Responses

Minimum (non-jump) responses in another suit are unlimited and demand a further bid by the opener. However, if the responder bids at the one level, the suit (a major) may be only four cards and the hand weak. Nevertheless, the suit may have five or more cards and the hand may be just below the level of strength required for a jump take-out. This dilemma may be resolved by making a jump raise of the responder's suit only when holding four cards. In this case a single jump shows 6 winners and a jump to game 6·2 winners.

Opener	Responder A	Responder B
♠ KQxx	♠ AJxx	♠ AJxx
13/6 ♥ AQxxx	7/3 ♥ Jx	10/4 ♥ Jx
♦ x	♦ Jxxx	♦ Jxxx
♣ Qxx	♣ xxx	♣ Kxx
	6 + 3 = 9	6 + 4 = 10

Bidding A	1♥	1♠	Bidding B	1♥	1♠
	3♠	Pass		3♠	4♠

With only three-card support for the major suit response and a hand near the top of the opening bid range, bid either 2NT or another suit rather than give jump support. With a weaker hand, partner's suit may be supported:

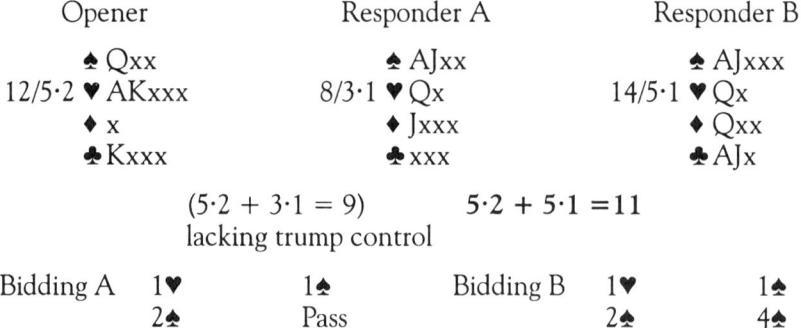

	Opener	Responder A	Responder B
	♠ Qxx	♠ AJxx	♠ AJxxx
12/5·2	♥ AKxxx	8/3·1 ♥ Qx	14/5·1 ♥ Qx
	♦ x	♦ Jxxx	♦ Qxx
	♣ Kxxx	♣ xxx	♣ AJx

$$(5·2 + 3·1 = 9) \qquad 5·2 + 5·1 = 11$$
lacking trump control

Bidding A	1♥	1♠	Bidding B	1♥	1♠
	2♠	Pass		2♠	4♠

When lacking even three-card support for responder's suit, the choice of rebid lies between bidding one's own suit again (six-card suit), bidding an alternative suit, or with 5,3,3,2 distribution bidding No Trumps (13-15 bid 1NT, 16, 17 bid 2NT).

We follow the normal practice that bids of our own or partner's suit are always limit bids up to the full value of the hand, as are most bids of No Trumps.

If the response is at the two level in a minor suit, hand shape should be shown by the opener by bidding an alternative major or No Trumps at the appropriate level (13-15 bid 2NT, 16, 17 bid 3NT). A minimum rebid of the opening suit could indicate a misfit or a weak hand with a six-card suit.

Response is 2♦ to an opening 1♠ bid. Rebid:

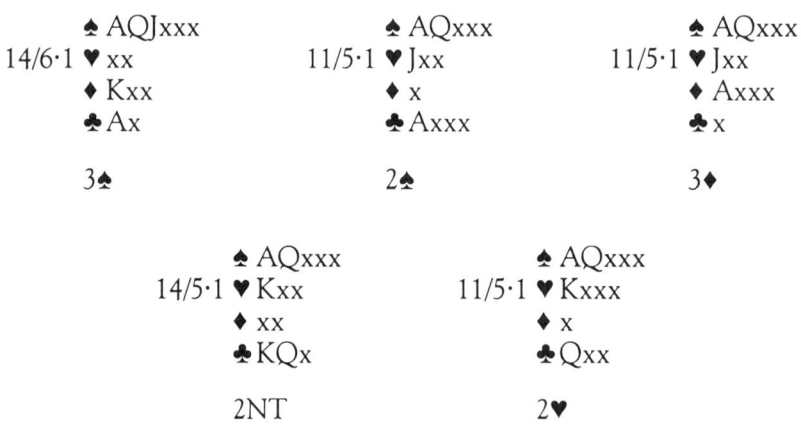

	♠ AQJxxx	♠ AQxxx	♠ AQxxx
14/6·1	♥ xx	11/5·1 ♥ Jxx	11/5·1 ♥ Jxx
	♦ Kxx	♦ x	♦ Axxx
	♣ Ax	♣ Axxx	♣ x
	3♠	2♠	3♦

	♠ AQxxx	♠ AQxxx
14/5·1	♥ Kxx	11/5·1 ♥ Kxxx
	♦ xx	♦ x
	♣ KQx	♣ Qxx
	2NT	2♥

All except the first hand would raise a 2♥ response to three.

When holding a little better than a minimum hand, do not be afraid to reverse (a reverse bid is a rebid that forces partner to choose your original suit at the three level), since your opening bid has already limited your hand.

	Opener	Responder A	Responder B
	♠ Kxxx	♠ Axxx	♠ Axx
12/5·2	♥ xx	11/5·1 ♥ Axx	9/4·2 ♥ Qxxx
	♦ AQxxx	♦ x	♦ x
	♣ Kx	♣ QJxxx	♣ QJxxx

$$5·2 + 5·1 = 11 \qquad (5·2 + 4·2 = 10·1)$$
$$\text{lacking trump control}$$

Bidding A	1♦	2♣	Bidding B	1♦	2♣
	2♠	4♠		2♠	Pass

On the rebid of spades, Responder B knows there is no hope of game and passes at the lowest level in the seven-card spade suit.

When partner makes a jump take-out, which is forcing to game and a slam invitation, we need to know whether his bid is based on support for our suit, his own powerful suit, or general strength. We should normally make the lowest meaningful bid to allow him to elucidate. The subsequent course of bidding will depend on your favoured slam conventions. For example, using Blackwood:

	Opener	Responder A	Responder B
	♠ xx	♠ AKxx	♠ AKQxxx
12/5·2	♥ AQxxx	16/7 ♥ Kxxx	16/7 ♥ Kx
	♦ AQxx	♦ x	♦ xx
	♣ xx	♣ AQxx	♣ Axx

$$5·2 + 7 = 12·2 \qquad 5·2 + 7 = 12·2$$

Bidding A	1♥	2♠	Bidding B	1♥	2♠
	3♦	3♥		3♦	3♠
	4NT	5♥		4♠	4NT
	6♥	Pass		5♥	6♠

Optional Extras

i) Opening Bids

We can take a relaxed view of the 10-point minimum if the winners exceed 5. E.g.,

Open 1♠ on:

♠ AQJxxx	♥ xx	♦ Qxxx	♣ x	9/5·2

Also, some 5,3,3,2 hands with a major suit should be bid with 12 points but only 4·2 winners, e.g.,

♠ AQJxx   ♥ KQx   ♦ xx   ♣ xxx   12/4·2

The small lack of winners is compensated by the decreased probability of duplication of values with partner with this distribution.

When one is the third bidder, it pays to open light with the object of obstructing the fourth bidder, who would otherwise be expected to open. Such a bid should only be made with a good suit to indicate a lead if we lose the auction. E.g., bid 1♠ with:

♠ KQJxxx   ♥ xx   ♦ Jxx   ♣ xx   7/4

ii) **Responses**

When the responder has 7 or 8 points and a 4,4,4,1 hand with the singleton in his partner's suit, he can bid a major unless the suit is spades. In this case, the risk of passing and missing a good fit in another suit is too great and he should bid 1NT although nominally below strength. The opener will only rebid spades if he has 6.

If the opener has a second suit of hearts, it may even be possible to bid to game.

15/6·2	♠ AKxxx	8/4·1	♠ x
	♥ KQxx		♥ Axxx
	♦ Kx		♦ Axxx
	♣ xx		♣ xxxx

$$6·2 + 4·1 = 11$$

Bidding	1♠	1NT
	2♥	3♥
	4♥	Pass

CHAPTER FOUR:
THE PHONEY CLUB
("WEAK" 1♣)

Requirements for Opening 1♣

As we have seen in Part One, it is necessary to open the bidding with any hand which has 13 or more points to avoid missing a game in 3 No Trumps. The opening bid chosen for minimum (13-15 point) hands with no five-card suit (4,4,3,2 or 4,3,3,3 or 4,4,4,1 hands) is 1♣. This opening bid can allow the bidding to stop at 1 of a major suit and thus avoid the danger of being doubled in 1NT.

Since it is desirable to bid 1♣ with many hands containing a five-card or longer club suit, it is necessary to follow a careful procedure to distinguish between the various types of hands opening 1♣. It is also important to preserve the limited nature of the bidding sequences. In other words, we must avoid the lazy practice of opening almost any type of hand with 1♣.

Because the short suit hands of 13-15 points are much more common than the other hands using the 1♣ opener, it is assumed that the bid means this type of hand, until contrary information is given in subsequent bidding.

Typical 1♣ hands are:

	♠ AJxx		♠ x		♠ AQx		♠ xx
13/5	♥ Qxx	15/6·2	♥ KQxx	13/4	♥ Kxxx	13/5	♥ KQxx
	♦ KQxx		♦ AQxx		♦ Jxx		♦ KQx
	♣ Jx		♣ Axxx		♣ Kxx		♣ Kxxx

Weak 1♣ openers have from 4 to 6·2 winners.

Opening 1♣ with a Club Suit

The priority use for the 1♣ opener is that shown on the previous page. The bid promises a minimum of 13 points. Any 13 or more point hand with a five-card club suit should also open 1♣ unless it is suitable for a 1NT bid (5,3,3,2 with 16 or 17 points — as with the diamond suit discussed in Chapter Three) or strong enough to open 2♣.

Examples showing when to use or not to use the 1♣ opener:

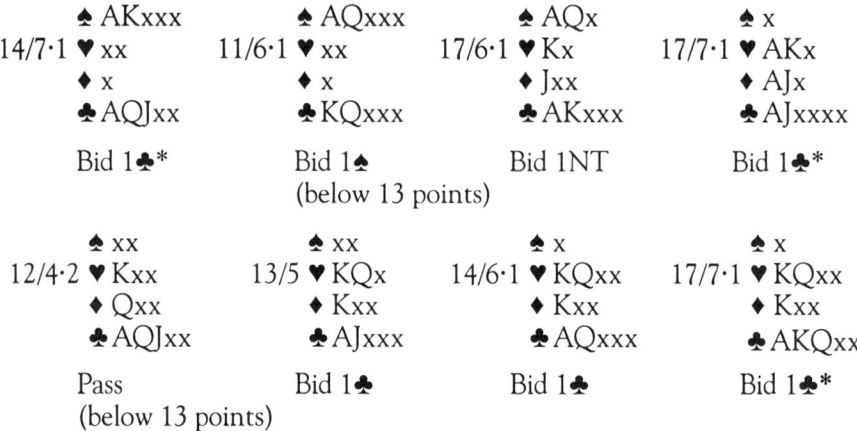

♠ AKxxx	♠ AQxxx	♠ AQx	♠ x
14/7·1 ♥ xx	11/6·1 ♥ xx	17/6·1 ♥ Kx	17/7·1 ♥ AKx
♦ x	♦ x	♦ Jxx	♦ AJx
♣ AQJxx	♣ KQxxx	♣ AKxxx	♣ AJxxxx
Bid 1♣*	Bid 1♠	Bid 1NT	Bid 1♣*
	(below 13 points)		

♠ xx	♠ xx	♠ x	♠ x
12/4·2 ♥ Kxx	13/5 ♥ KQx	14/6·1 ♥ KQxx	17/7·1 ♥ KQxx
♦ Qxx	♦ Kxx	♦ Kxx	♦ Kxx
♣ AQJxx	♣ AJxxx	♣ AQxxx	♣ AKQxx
Pass	Bid 1♣	Bid 1♣	Bid 1♣*
(below 13 points)			

Such 1♣ hands have from 5 to 8·2 winners but are divided into strong hands (18 or more points or 7 or more winners) or normal "one suit" openers (5 to 6·2 winners) by subsequent bidding. The hands marked * are examples of the "strong" 1♣.

Requirements for Responses

Responses to 1♣

Although the opener is expected to be weak, the bid is absolutely forcing for one round. If the responder cannot make a positive response, he bids 1♦.

Usual positive responses are of two kinds — either limited responses at the one level, or forcing responses at the two level. As is usual in this system, the suit bids show a five-card or longer suit, while the NT bids deny a five-card major.

Limited Responses

There are just three limited positive responses — 1♠, 1♥ and 1NT. Responses of 1♠ or 1♥ are made with suited hands of 3 - 4·2 winners (maximum points 11). The response 1NT shows 9 - 11 points and no five-card major. They are therefore similar to responses to 1♠, 1♥ and 1♦. We do not have to memorise a different set of points or minimum winners. Examples of responses to 1♣:

	♠ Jxxxx		♠ AQxxx		♠ Axx		♠ Axx
7/3	♥ xx	10/4	♥ xx	10/4	♥ xx	10/4	♥ xx
	♦ Axx		♦ Axx		♦ Kxxx		♦ Jxx
	♣ Qxx		♣ xxx		♣ Kxxx		♣ KQxxx
	Bid 1♠		Bid 1♠		Bid 1NT		Bid 1NT

Forcing Responses

The responder does not know where his partner's strength lies and has to assume initially that he may have only 13 points. He would be unwise to take the bidding to the two level unless strong.

We use *all two level responses* as game forces; 2NT for non-suited hands and 5,3,3,2 hands with a minor suit, and the other two bids for suited hands. The minimum requirement for all these bids is 12 points, or for major suits, 5 winners with 10 points. That is, the minimum requirement is roughly equivalent to that for an opening bid. The bids are unlimited, and especially in the case of suit bids may lead to a slam attempt when there is a fit.

Note that the forcing response 2♣ does not sound strong, and it is important to remember that both minor suit 2 bids are strength-showing.

Examples of forcing responses to 1♣:

	♠ KJx		♠ AQxxx		♠ AQxxx		♠ Kxxx
12/3·2	♥ Kxx	12/4·2	♥ xx	10/6	♥ KJxxx	13/6	♥ QJx
	♦ Qxxx		♦ AQx		♦ xx		♦ AKxxx
	♣ Kxx		♣ xxx		♣ x		♣ x
	Bid 2NT		Bid 2♣		Bid 2♠		Bid 2♦

	♠ Ax		♠ Kxx		♠ x		♠ Kxxx
16/7	♥ KQJxxx	13/5	♥ QJx	14/6·1	♥ Axx	13/6	♥ AQxx
	♦ Kx		♦ AKxxx		♦ Axx		♦ x
	♣ Kxx		♣ xx		♣ AQxxxx		♣ Axxx
	Bid 2♥		Bid 2NT		Bid 2♣		Bid 2NT
	slam possibility						

25

Negative Response

The compulsory 1♦ response is made on any hand which does not qualify for a positive response. All the following hands should bid 1♦. There is no implication about distribution, and 1♦ may be bid when holding a diamond suit, but not strong enough for a positive bid of 1NT or a forcing bid of 2♦.

Examples of the 1♦ negative response:

```
          ♠ KQxxx              ♠ x                 ♠ Qxx
5/2·1     ♥ xx      5/3·1      ♥ xxx     8/2·1     ♥ Qxxx
          ♦ xxx                ♦ AJxxxx            ♦ Qxx
          ♣ xxx                ♣ xxx               ♣ Qxx

          ♠ xxx                ♠ Kxxx
8/3·1     ♥ Axx     7/4        ♥ x
          ♦ xx                 ♦ Qxxx
          ♣ KJxxx              ♣ Qxxx
```

The same response is made with a worthless hand. Hands like those shown may find a bid on the next round.

Higher Jump Responses

Higher suit responses show a long suit and are two-way bids. 3 or 4 of a major and 4 of a minor combine the shut out value of a barrier bid with the hope of game if there is a fit with partner. The 3 bids require 4 winners and the 4 bids 5 or more winners. The response of 3 in a minor suggests a 3NT contract and is made when holding a long strong suit with a little outside strength if there is a loser in it.

```
          ♠ AQxxxx             ♠ AQxxxxx           ♠ xx                ♠ KQx
8/4·1     ♥ x        8/5·1     ♥ x        10/5     ♥ Ax      8/5·1     ♥ xx
          ♦ Qxx                ♦ Qxx                ♦ xxx               ♦ x
          ♣ xxx                ♣ xx                 ♣ KQJxxx            ♣ QJxxxxx

          Bid 3♠               Bid 4♠               Bid 3♣              Bid 4♣
```

A response of 3NT to 1♣ requires the same as in response to 1♠, etc. (4,3,3 with 15 or 16 points).

26

Rebids by 1♣ Opener

A rebid of clubs shows a five-card or longer club suit, but it may not always be advisable to do this. Four-card suits are normally bid in the most economical order, and hearts are bid before spades.

After the 1♦ Response

After the negative response, the partnership will have between 13 and 23 points — median 19. The main consideration for a weak 1♣ opener is safety. He must avoid a bid at the two level, which would mean he is in the strong 1♣ bracket of at least 18 points or 7 winners. He seeks the lowest viable contract by bidding a four-card major (1♥ if he has both). With no four-card major but with four or more clubs, he bids 1NT. If diamonds is his only suit, he must pass the 1♦ response. If this is doubled, the responder can choose the best contract knowing the exact distribution. See also Chapter Ten. For example, the rebids are:

	♠ AKxx		♠ xx		♠ Axx		♠ Axx
14/5·1	♥ Jxxx	15/5·2	♥ Kxx	14/4·1	♥ Kxx	14/4·1	♥ Kxx
	♥ xx		♦ KQx		♦ Qxxx		♦ AJx
	♣ AQx		♣ AKxxx		♣ AJx		♣ Qxxx
	Bid 1♥		Bid 1NT		Pass		Bid 1NT

Rebids of 2 of a suit show strength and therefore a five-card or longer club suit, as well as at least five cards in the suit bid. The two-suiter will have 7 or more winners, while a rebid of 2♣ shows either 7 or more winners or 18 or more points. After the partner's negative response, it is rather like opening with a 2 bid as in Chapter Six. For example, rebid:

	♠ AKxxx		♠ x		♠ xx
14/7·1	♥ xx	17/7·1	♥ AKx	13/5	♥ KQx
	♦ x		♦ AJx		♦ Kxx
	♣ AQJxx		♣ AJxxxx		♣ AJxxx
	Bid 2♠		Bid 2♣		Bid 1NT

	♠ x		♠ x
17/7·1	♥ KQxx	14/6·1	♥ KQxx
	♦ Kxx		♦ Kxx
	♣ AKQxx		♣ AQxxx
	Bid 2♣		Bid 1♥

In the fourth example a rebid of 2♥ would show five or more hearts, so the strength showing bid is 2♣. The 1♥ rebid in the fifth example shows four hearts.

Rebids After the Limited Positive Responses 1NT, 1♠, 1♥

These responses do not require any further bid from the opener unless he has values either in points or winners above the minimum. For example, a 13 point hand opposite even the highest hand for a 1NT response — 11 points — could not produce the necessary 25 points for 3NT. Over the 1NT response, it is only worth bidding when holding 15 (sometimes 14) points or a four-card major suit with a distributional winner.

If the opener has support for his partner's major, he should proceed on a count of winners, passing with less than 5 winners or 15 points. With 5 - 5·2 winners he bids 2, with 6-6·1 winners 3, and with 6·2 winners 4. In each case he assumes 3 winners for partner (3 + 5 = 8, etc.). Similarly, partner can continue if he has extra values.

When lacking support for the suit bid in response to 1♣, it is necessary to be cautious. With 4,4,4,1 distribution and a singleton opposite a 1♥ bid, it is obviously right to bid 1♠ in the hope of finding a 4 - 3 or 4 - 4 fit in either spades or a minor. Any 15-point hand can continue the bidding with 1NT, which does not imply a club suit over the positive response.

Examples of rebids:

	♠ Axx	♠ Kxxx	♠ AQx	♠ Kx
13/5	♥ xx	13/6 ♥ x	15/4·2 ♥ Kxx	13/6 ♥ Qxx
	♦ Axxx	♦ Axxx	♦ Kxxx	♦ Ax
	♣ AJxx	♣ AQxx	♣ Kxx	♣ Axxxxx

Pass 1NT or 1♥	Bid 1♠ over 1♥	Bid 1NT over 1♠	Raise 1♥ to 3
Raise 1♠ to 2	Raise 1♠ to 3	or 1♥	Bid 2♣ over 1♠
	Bid 2♦ over 1NT	Raise 1NT to 2	or 1NT

Many 14-point hands present borderline problems which may be resolved by considering the intermediate cards — tens and nines.

When the opener has a strong club hand (7 or more winners or 18 points) with one or more five-card suits, he must indicate this by a jump bid over the limited positive response.

	♠ AKxxx		♠ xx		♠ xx
14/7·1	♥ x	17/7·1	♥ AKxx	19/7	♥ Axx
	♦ xx		♦ Kx		♦ AQx
	♣ AQJxx		♣ AQJxx		♣ AKQxx

Bid 3♠ over 1NT	Bid 3♣ over	Bid 3♣ over 1♥
Bid 2♠ over 1♥	1NT or 1♠	or 1NT
	Bid 4♣ over 1♥	Bid 2NT over 1♠

The 4♣ rebids are cue bids which, by inference, show the club suit and good support for partner's suit. All the rebids show the club suit, although with the 2NT bid in example three it might be only four clubs (see strong 4,4,4,1 hands to follow).

Rebids After a Two Level Response (Game Force)

The priority is to show distribution, keeping the bidding low where there is a choice. Minimum suit bids other than ♣ show four cards, while a jump bid shows a strong ♣. Such a jump should not normally be made over a suit response if it takes the bidding to the four level. The same message about suit length may be given by repeating the suit.

Examples of rebids over two level responses:

♠ AKxx	♠ Kxx	♠ Kxxx	♠ x
14/5·1 ♥ xx	14 pts ♥ Kxx	14/6·1 ♥ x	16/8 ♥ AKxxx
♦ AQxx	♦ AJx	♦ AQx	♦ Kx
♣ Jxx	♣ QJxx	♣ AJxxx	♣ AQxxx

Bid 2♦ over 2♣	Bid 2NT over	Bid 2♠ over 2♥	Bid 3♥ over 2♠
Bid 2♠ over 2♥	any 2 suit	2♦ or 2♣	2♦ or 2♠
or 2♦	Bid 3NT over	Bid 3♣ over	Bid 4♥ over 2NT
Bid 3♦ over	2NT	2NT or 2♠	Bid 4♣ over 2♥
2NT or 2♠			(cue bid)

In the fourth example, the shape of the hand can be revealed after the 2♠ response by repeating ♥, showing that it is a five-card suit.

Opening 3♣

This bid is reserved for hands too weak in points to open 1♣, but holding a good six- or seven-card suit. Partner with all-around strength will convert to 3NT but, the bid is in any case a barrier to the opponents.

♠ x	♠ Kx	♠ Kx	♠ Kx
11/5·1 ♥ Qxx	12/6·2 ♥ Qx	14/6·1 ♥ Qx	12/5·2 ♥ Qx
♦ Qxx	♦ xx	♦ Axx	♦ Kxx
♣ AQJxxx	♣ AKxxxx	♣ KQxxx	♣ KJxxxx

Bid 3♣	Bid 3♣	Bid 1♣	Pass

In the fourth example, the clubs are not good enough for the 3♣ opener. There may be an opportunity to bid later.

An opening bid of 4♣ is like any other pre-emptive bid (Chapter Eight).

4,4,4,1 Hands

As we have seen 4,4,4,1 hands with 13 - 15 points fall naturally into the definition of weak 1♣ hands. There is, however, a problem in this system for 4,4,4,1 hands of 16 - 22 points, since they cannot be opened with a suit bid or NT. The answer is to make use of the forcing nature of the 1♣ opener for such hands. The stronger (20 - 22 point) hands can be shown by jumping in NT when partner does not choose one of our three suits, or bids the negative 1♦. A weak 1♣ opener could not do this. The 2NT bid over 1♦, like an opening 2NT, is not forcing.

Two examples:

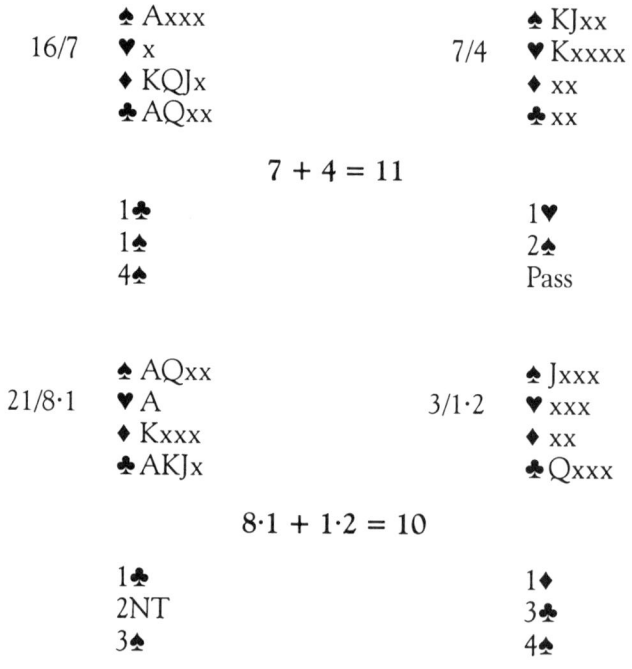

	♠ Axxx			♠ KJxx
16/7	♥ x		7/4	♥ Kxxxx
	♦ KQJx			♦ xx
	♣ AQxx			♣ xx

$$7 + 4 = 11$$

1♣		1♥
1♠		2♠
4♠		Pass

	♠ AQxx			♠ Jxxx
21/8·1	♥ A		3/1·2	♥ xxx
	♦ Kxxx			♦ xx
	♣ AKJx			♣ Qxxx

$$8·1 + 1·2 = 10$$

1♣		1♦
2NT		3♣
3♠		4♠

The 3♣ bid is based on an interest in a major, in this case spades. When the opener bids 3♠, his singleton must be in hearts, so it is clear that the hands fit. If the responder's spades and hearts were exchanged, he could pass the 3♠ bid.

Further Examples of Bidding After the 1♣ Opener

Opener		Responder A		Responder B	
	♠ Kxx		♠ xx		♠ xxx
14/5·1	♥ Ax	6/2·2	♥ Kxxx	7/3	♥ KJxxx
	♦ KJxx		♦ xxx		♦ xx
	♣ Kxxx		♣ QJxx		♣ QJx

5·1 + 2·2 = 8		14 + 7 = 21 points	
Bidding A		Bidding B	
1♣	1♦	1♣	1♥
1NT	2♣	1NT	Pass

The 1NT rebid over 1♦ shows 4 or more clubs. Opposite Responder B there is still hope of 3NT if responder has 11 points.

Opener		Responder C		Responder D	
	♠ Kxx		♠ AQxxx		♠ QJx
14/5·1	♥ Ax	9/3·2	♥ xxx	11/4·1	♥ Kxxx
	♦ KJxx		♦ Qx		♦ Ax
	♣ Kxxx		♣ Jxx		♣ Jxxx

5·1 + 3·2 = 9		14 + 11 = 25 points	
Bidding C		Bidding D	
1♣	1♠	1♣	1NT
2♣	Pass	2NT	3NT

Opener		Responder A		Responder B	
	♠ AKxxx		♠ Qxx		♠ xx
15/7·2	♥ x	5/2·1	♥ Jxxxx	7/3	♥ KQxxx
	♦ Kx		♦ Qxx		♦ Qxx
	♣ AJxxx		♣ xx		♣ xxx

7·2 + 2·1 = 10		7·2 + 3 = 10·2	
Bidding A		Bidding B	
1♣	1♦	1♣	1♥
2♠	3♠	2♠	3♣
4♠	Pass	Pass	

When Responder A raises the 2♠ bid on a count of winners, the opener with extra values raises to four. Responder B's bid of 3♣ showing preference at the lowest level makes a game unlikely.

Opener		Responder A		Responder B	
	♠ AQxx		♠ Kxx		♠ Kx
14/5·1	♥ xx	6/2·2	♥ Jxxxx	15/6·2	♥ Kx
	♦ KJxx		♦ Qxx		♦ AQxxxx
	♣ Axx		♣ xx		♣ Kxx

(5·1 + 2·2 = 8)		5·1 + 6·2 = 12	
Bidding A		Bidding B	
1♣	1♦	1♣	2♦
1♠	Pass	2♠	2NT
		3♦	4NT
		5♥	6♦

With Responder A, the partnership is happy to settle in the safe contract of 1♠. Responder B chooses 2NT to protect his kings, but on hearing the mild slam suggestion of 3♦, instead of closing at 3NT, he initiates a Blackwood sequence.

Opener		Responder A		Responder B	
	♠ x		♠ Axx		♠ KQxx
16/8	♥ AKxxx	13/5	♥ Qxxxx	12/4·2	♥ xx
	♦ Kx		♦ Axx		♦ Axxx
	♣ AQxxx		♣ Kx		♣ Kxx

8 + 5 = 13		8 + 4·2 = 12·2	
Bidding A		Bidding B	
1♣	2♥	1♣	2NT
4♣	5NT	4♥	5♣
7♥	Pass	6♣	Pass

With Responder A, the 4♣ cue bid shows the two-suiter and enables partner to use the 5NT Grand Slam Force to locate two of the top three trumps. Responder B chooses between the two suits offered, enabling his partner with extra values to bid the slam.

Opener		Responder	
	♠ Kxx		♠ QJxx
13/5	♥ Axxx	5/2·1	♥ xx
	♦ Qxxx		♦ xxx
	♣ Ax		♣ Qxxx

Bidding	
1♣	1♦
1♥	1♠

The responder knows they only have six hearts, so he tries spades.

Optional Extra

When holding a five-card or longer club suit and a four-card major, 1♣ can be opened with only 12 points.

CHAPTER FIVE:
OPENING BIDS IN NO TRUMPS

The Strong No Trump

Among the most profitable of business doubles is the double of an injudicious 1NT. Systems incorporating a weak 1NT automatically employ a potentially injudicious 1NT. So do those using a weak 1NT response. They usually, but not invariably, escape punishment because of the unknown strength of the hand partnering the 1NT bidder. Systems employing a variable opening NT according to vulnerability in effect combine two different systems, thus stretching the memory and judgment of their followers.

This system uses a strong NT of 16 - 19 points and 4,4,3,2 or 4,3,3,3 distribution. The bid is also used for 5,3,3,2 distribution with a five-card minor and 16 or 17 points. The stronger (18 or 19 points) hands are distinguished from the weaker (16 or 17 points) hands on the next round of bidding when significant. This means that the uncertainty is no greater after the second round of bidding than with systems which limit the spread of points for a 1NT opener to only three. Examples of 1NT hands:

	♠ Axx		♠ AKx		♠ Qxx		♠ xx
16/5	♥ Kxx	19/7	♥ Kx	17/6·1	♥ Ax	17/6·1	♥ AKxx
	♦ QJxx		♦ QJxx		♦ KQxxx		♦ QJx
	♣ AQx		♣ AQxx		♣ AQx		♣ AKxx

1NT openers have from 5 - 7 winners.

Responses to 1NT

This opening bid is not forcing and should be passed with a poor hand that cannot make one of the following positive responses. These distinguish between suited hands and those which have no five-card suit other than clubs.

Minimum Suit Response — 2♠ 2♥ 2♦

The 2♣ response is used for non-suited hands of 6 - 8 points as well as for some hands with a club suit — more about this later.

The range of strength for the three minimum bids on suited hands is from 2·2 winners with 6 points or 3 winners up to 4·2 winners. The bids are forcing for one round. The weaker hands are shown by rebidding the suit (distress rebid).

Jump Suit Response — Three of Any Suit

These bids are forcing to game and are made on suited hands with 5 or more winners or 12 points.

2♣ Response

This is the minimum positive response with a non-suited hand or a club suit and requires 6 - 8 points. It is normally forcing for one round and may lead to a game contract if the opener is in the higher range, or if a major suit fit is found. This usage is similar to, but of greater age than, the Stayman Convention which may have the same effect. However, it does not promise a four-card major.

Responses in NT

2NT shows 9 - 14 points with no five-card major and is forcing to game.

3NT (15 or 16 points) requires a slam contract if the opener has 18 or 19 points.

Stronger non-suit hands can be bid as a direct 4NT leading to a search for a suit fit, or straight to 6NT.

Examples of Responses to 1NT:

♠ Jxx	♠ Qxxx	♠ xx	♠ QJxxx
6/2·2 ♥ xx	6/2·2 ♥ xx	5/2·1 ♥ Qxxxx	6/2·2 ♥ xx
♦ xxx	♦ Qxxx	♦ Qxx	♦ Kxx
♣ KQxxx	♣ Qxx	♣ Jxx	♣ xxx
Bid 2♣	Bid 2♣	Pass	Bid 2♠

♠ Qxxxxx	♠ Ax	♠ Kxx	♠ Axxx
4/3 ♥ x	9/3·2 ♥ Jxx	9/2·2 ♥ Kxx	9/3·2 ♥ Kxxx
♦ Qxx	♦ Qxx	♦ Kxxx	♦ Qx
♣ xxx	♣ Qxxxx	♣ xxx	♣ xxx
Bid 2♠	Bid 2NT	Bid 2NT	Bid 2NT then
Repeat ♠	then 3NT	then 3NT	support a major
unless	or pass 3NT	or pass 3NT	or bid 3♥
supported			unless opener
			bids 3NT

♠ xx	♠ x	♠ Axxxx	♠ Axxx
9/4·2 ♥ xx	13/6 ♥ Axx	9/4·2 ♥ Kxxx	11/5·1 ♥ KQxxx
♦ KQxxxx	♦ Kxx	♦ x	♦ x
♣ Axx	♣ AQxxxx	♣ Qxx	♣ Qxx
Bid 2♦	Bid 3♣	Bid 2♠	Bid 3♥
then 3NT			

Rebids by 1NT Opener

Rebids have two priorities — to indicate whether a four-card major suit is held, and to show the point strength as either minimum (16 or 17 points) or maximum (18 or 19 points).

If the response is 2♣, the higher point count is shown by jumping to 3 of a major or 3NT, and the lower point count by making any two bid (not forcing). With both majors, bid hearts at the appropriate level. When the opening NT is based on a five card minor, the point count is limited to 16 or 17. With 17 points and good prospects of 3NT, if partner has a suitable 7 or 8 points, 3♦ or 3♣ may be bid (not forcing). A rebid of 2♦ and exceptionally a pass of 2♣ or rebid of 2NT would show minimum hands.

Examples

Examples of Rebids over 2♣ Response

♠ KQx	♠ KQx	♠ Axxx	♠ AQxx
16/5 ♥ Axx	18/6·2 ♥ Ax	17/6·1 ♥ Ax	19/7 ♥ Ax
♦ Kxxx	♦ KQxx	♦ KJx	♦ KQx
♣ Axx	♣ Axxx	♣ AJxx	♣ Axxx
Bid 2NT	Bid 3NT	Bid 2♠	Bid 3♠
			(forcing)

♠ KJxx	♠ Ax	♠ Kx	♠ Ax
18/6·2 ♥ KJxx	16/6 ♥ Kxx	17/6·1 ♥ QJx	16/6 ♥ AJx
♦ AQx	♦ KQxxx	♦ QJx	♦ KQx
♣ Ax	♣ KJx	♣ AKJxx	♣ Qxxxx
Bid 3♥ (forcing)	Bid 2♦	Bid 3♣	Pass

Bidding After the 2NT Response

After the 2NT response there may be a slam if both hands are maximum. A minimum opener should sign off in 3NT or bid 3 of a major when this may lead to a safer contract. A maximum opener with 4,4,3,2 distribution should bid his lower four-card suit.

Opener	Responder A	Responder B
♠ AQxx	♠ Kxx	♠ Kxxx
16/6 ♥ Ax	13/5 ♥ Kxxx	10/3 ♥ xxx
♦ KQx	♦ Ax	♦ Axx
♣ Jxxx	♣ Kxxx	♣ Kxx

6 + 5 = 11	6 + 3 + 1 = 10
(clubs)	(no duplication)
Bidding A	**Bidding B**

1NT	2NT	1NT	2NT
3♠	3NT	3♠	4♠

The 3♠ bids show a minimum hand not particularly suited to a NT contract. Responder A lacks spade support and corrects to 3NT. Responder B knows that there can be no duplication of values and prefers the safer 4♠ contract.

Opener	Responder A	Responder B
♠ AQxx	♠ Kxx	♠ Kxx
19/7 ♥ Ax	13/5 ♥ Kxxx	10/4 ♥ KJxx
♦ KQx	♦ Ax	♦ xx
♣ Axxx	♣ QJxx	♣ QJxx

7 + 5 = 12	7 + 4 = 11
Bidding A	**Bidding B**

1NT	2NT	1NT	2NT
3♣	3♥	3♣	3♥
3♠	5♣	3♠	3NT
6♣	Pass	Pass	

The 3♣ bids show the higher strength of the opener. Responder A has four points above the minimum and a good fit for clubs, and invites the slam by bidding 5♣.

Bidding After a Suit Response

When the response has been 2 of a major, an opener with trump support can proceed on a count of winners, allowing 3 for partner. Lacking support, he can bid the other major, or 2 or 3NT according to strength — the three level bid requiring 18 or 19 points. Over 2♦, he will bid 2 of a major or 2NT and await developments. Exceptionally, with an absolute maximum he could bid 3NT, which would discourage a distress rebid.

Opener	Responder A	Responder B
♠ KQx	♠ Jxxxx	♠ Jxx
18/6·2 ♥ Ax	7/3 ♥ Kxx	7/3 ♥ Kxxxx
♦ KQxx	♦ xxx	♦ xxx
♣ Axxx	♣ Kx	♣ Kx

6·2 + 3 = 9·2	18 + 7 = 25
Bidding A	Bidding B

1NT	2♠	1NT	2♥
4♠	Pass	3NT	Pass

If the opener were at the minimum points level with the same distribution, the bidding would end at a rebid of 3♠ (Responder A) or 2NT (Responder B).

The jump response may be the preliminary to a slam attempt, if a fit can be found and either partner is above the minimum level for his bid.

	♠ AJxx		♠ Kxxx
18/6·2	♥ Ax	11/5·1	♥ QJx
	♦ KQx		♦ AJxxx
	♣ Axxx		♣ x

$$6·2 + 5·1 = 12$$

1NT		3♦
3♠		4♠
5♣		6♠

The 4 - 4 fit is normally preferred as trumps for a slam contract, since the long cards from the 5 - 3 suit provide discards. Having a strong NT in the maximum range, the opener takes the initiative in the search for a slam by bidding above game.

Opening Bid 2NT

Stronger hands with the NT distributions (4,4,3,3, 4,4,3,2, and 5,3,3,2 with minor suit) are opened 2NT. The points limits are 20 - 22, and hands stronger than this are opened 2♣. This use of 2NT is common to many systems.

A 2NT opener has from 6·1 to 8 winners.

Since the opening bid is limited and there is not much bidding space below the game level, responsibility for further action rests with the responder. There is again no weak take-out, and lacking 3 points or if pointless a six-card major, the bid should be passed.

If the responder has no four-card or longer major suit, the best hope of game is in 3NT. This should be bid with as little as 4 points or even 3 points in a five-card minor suit. Interest in a major suit is indicated by bidding 3♣, while direct major suit bids show at least five cards. Bids of 3 in a major may be either a game try with a weak hand or the preliminary to a slam try.

A useful convention is to bid 4 of a major when Aceless but holding sufficient winners (about 5) for a conditional slam invitation. 4NT by the opener would then ask for Kings. A bid of 3♦ is also a slam suggestion, since a poor hand with diamonds as the only suit would bid 3NT or pass.

More positive slam invitations are either 4 in a minor with suited hands, or direct raises in NT to 4 or more with no five-card suit. The 4NT bid which is not forcing is made with 12 points and some suitable 11-point hands based on higher honours. The opener may accept the invitation to investigate further by bidding four-card suits from the bottom, or his five-card minor.

Opener	Responder A	Responder B
♠ AQx	♠ Kxx	♠ KJxxxx
21/7·2 ♥ Ax	12/3·2 ♥ KJx	9/4·2 ♥ KQx
♦ KQxx	♦ AJxx	♦ xx
♣ KQJx	♣ xxx	♣ xx

7·2 + 3·2 + 1 = 12·1	7·2 + 4·2 = 12·1
(no duplication)	
Bidding A	Bidding B

2NT	4NT	2NT	4♠
5♣	5♦	Pass	
6♦	Pass	Two Aces	
		missing	

Opening Bids of 3NT

Very strong balanced hands are opened 2♣, leaving 3NT for special use with long solid minor suits. The hope is that your partner will have enough scattered strength to pass, rather than start a rescue by bidding 4♣.

CHAPTER SIX:
OPENING BIDS OF TWO OF A SUIT
EXCEPT CLUBS

Requirements for Opening Two Bids

Bids of one of a suit are limited by using two bids for fairly strong suited hands. The required range of strength has already been given in Chapter Four on the "strong" 1♣. Such hands have about 7 or 8 winners, the minimum requirement being 7 winners or any 18 points — with a 5,3,3,2 hand, this is 6˙2 winners. There is a slight difference between the bid in a major suit and in diamonds, for two reasons. First, the stronger major suit hands more readily qualify for a 2♣ bid (forcing to game), and second, the minor suit hand is more likely to aim towards a 3NT game. The normal maximum for winners is 8˙1, but any hand of 23 points qualifies for 2♣. The points range is therefore from about 14 to 22, but of course winners are the main criterion.

Most of these hands are based on a number of distributional winners and have either a six-card suit or two five-card suits. In the latter case, if one of the suits is clubs, the opening bid should be 1♣. If not, the higher ranking suit should be bid, and this causes no problem when the suits are touching (spades/hearts or hearts/diamonds). Spades/diamonds, however, gives a problem if your partner replies in hearts. Minimum hands with a singleton heart should therefore avoid the 2♠ opener by bidding 1♠. The following examples will show these distinctions:

♠ AQJxx	♥ KQx	♦ AQx	♣ xx	18/6·2	open 2♠
♠ AJxx	♥ AKQxxx	♦ xx	♣ x	14/7·1	open 2♥
♠ x	♥ AQJxx	♦ xx	♣ AKJxx	15/7·2	open 1♣
♠ x	♥ KJxxx	♦ AKQxx	♣ Ax	17/8·1	open 2♥
♠ x	♥ AKJxxx	♦ KQJ	♣ AKx	21/8·2	open 2♣

This hand requires very little from partner for 10 tricks.

| ♠ AQxxx | ♥ x | ♦ AKxxx | ♣ Jx | 14/7·1 | open 1♠ |

A problem if partner replies 3♥ to 2♠.

| ♠ AKxxx | ♥ Jx | ♦ AQJxx | ♣ x | 15/7·2 | open 2♠ |

We can bid 4♦ over 3♥ and pass a 4♥ rebid. In this sequence the 4♦ bid is not a cue bid.

| ♠ AJxx | ♥ x | ♦ KQJxxx | ♣ Ax | 15/7·2 | open 2♦ |
| ♠ Kxx | ♥ x | ♦ AKQxxxx | ♣ Jx | 13/7 | open 3NT |

Requirements for Responses

Responses to 2♠ 2♥ 2♦

A. Weak Hands

These opening bids are limited, not forcing, and the responder needs some values to respond. With trump support for a major, proceed on a count of winners allowing 7 for the opener. That is, raise to 3 with 2 to 2·1 winners and to 4 with 2·2 to 3·2 winners. Opposite 2♦ only, a four-card major with a stop should be shown when holding 6 or more points. Any five-card major may also be shown, but care should be exercised with minor suits. 3♣ has a special use.

As previously discussed, we should avoid bidding NT with a weak hand, and we substitute a bid of 3♣ for balanced hands with 6 - 8 points, as with the 2♣ response to 1NT. This bid is, of course, forcing for one round and is also used when holding a five-card club suit and 6 or more points.

	♠ xxx		♠ Kxxx		♠ xx		♠ Jxx
4/2	♥ xx	7/3	♥ xx	7/3	♥ QJxxx	8/3·1	♥ xx
	♦ Jxx		♦ Jxx		♦ Kxx		♦ xxx
	♣ Kxxxx		♣ Kxxx		♣ Jxx		♣ AKxxx

over 2♠ bid 3♠	over 2♠ bid 4♠	over 2♠ bid 3♥	over 2♠ bid 4♠
over 2♥ pass	over 2♥ bid 3♣	over 2♥ bid 4♥	over 2♥ bid 3♣
over 2♦ bid 3♦	over 2♦ bid 2♠	over 2♦ bid 2♥	over 2♦ bid 3♣

B. Stronger Hands

Balanced hands of 9 or more points have the choice of bidding 3NT or supporting the opening bid. For some awkward hands the 3♣ bid is also available.

	♠ xx		♠ xx		♠ xxx		♠ xx
9/3·2	♥ Kxxx	10/4	♥ KQxx	11/3·1	♥ Kxxx	11/4·1	♥ Kxx
	♦ Kxx		♦ xxx		♦ KJx		♦ KQxx
	♣ Kxxx		♣ KQxx		♣ KJx		♣ QJxx

over 2♠ bid 3NT	over 2♠ bid 3♣	over 2♠ bid 3NT	over 2♠ bid 3NT
over 2♥ bid 4♥	over 2♥ bid 3♣	over 2♥ bid 4♥	over 2♥ bid 3♣
over 2♦ bid 2♥	over 2♦ bid 2♥	over 2♦ bid 2♥	over 2♦ bid 3♣

When the 3♣ bid is made with trump support, a subsequent raise of the opener's suit shows a hand of 4 or more winners. This may lead to a slam.

Stronger hands with long suits are bid naturally unless they qualify for one of the special bids in the optional section below.

Optional Extras

1. Jump Response in 3♠ or 3♥

These jumps show at least a good six-card suit with little outside value. E.g., bid 3♠ over 2♥ or 2♦ with:

♠ KQJxxx	♥ xx	♦ xx	♣ Qxx	8/4·1

2. Slam Invitation — 2NT

So far, 2NT is an idle bid and it has been found valuable to use it for a slam invitation when holding trump support, a good hand, and two Norman points (Ace = 1, King = ½). We also allow ½ point for a singleton on suitable hands. The bid can be made on both suited and non-suited hands of about 5 or more winners. E.g., bid 2NT over 2♥ with:

♠ KQx	♥ xxx	♦ AKxx	♣ Kxx	15/4·2
♠ Ax	♥ xxxx	♦ AQxxx	♣ xx	10/5
♠ AKx	♥ Qxxx	♦ x	♣ QJxxx	12/5·2

When this convention is used, responses to the Blackwood 4NT by the opener are modified:

Responses

5♣	2 Norman points
5♦	2 ½ Norman points
5♥	3 Norman points

Example

	♠ Kxx		♠ Ax
19/7	♥ KQJxx	10/5	♥ xxxx
	♦ Kxx		♦ AQxxx
	♣ AK		♣ xx

$$7 + 5 = 12$$

2♥	2NT
3NT	4♦
4NT	5♣
6♥	Pass

One Ace is known to be missing. The slam is bid in hearts to protect the spade King from attack by the opening lead.

3. Conditional Slam Suggestion After 2♠ and 2♥ Opener

When holding trump support but lacking the two Norman points for the 2NT response, a conditional slam invitation can be made in 4♦ or 4♣. At least 4 winners and 1½ Norman points are necessary. Over 2♠, bid as follows:

♠ Kxxx	♥ xx	♦ AJxx	♣ QJx	11/4·1	Bid 4♦
♠ xxxx	♥ xx	♦ xx	♣ AKQxx	9/4·2	Bid 4♣
♠ Kxx	♥ xx	♦ AQxxxx	♣ xx	9/4·2	Bid 4♦

	♠ AQJxx		♠ Kxx
17/7·1	♥ AQJx	9/4·2	♥ xx
	♦ Kx		♦ AQxxxx
	♣ xx		♣ xx

$$7·1 + 4·2 = 12$$

2♠	4♦
4♠	Pass

The declarer knows that two Aces or one Ace and two Kings are missing.

Further Examples of Bidding After 2♠ 2♥ 2♦ Opener

Opener	Responder A	Responder B
♠ x	♠ KQJxxx	♠ Axx
17/8·1 ♥ KJxxx	8/4·1 ♥ xx	11/4·1 ♥ Qxxx
♦ AKQxx	♦ xx	♦ xx
♣ Ax	♣ Qxx	♣ KQxx

(No fit) 　　　　　　　　　　　　　8·1 + 4·1 = 12·2

2♥	3♠	2♥	4♣
4♠	Pass	4♦	4♥
(Points above minimum)		6♥	Pass

Opener	Responder C	Responder D
♠ x	♠ QJxx	♠ Jxxx
17/8·1 ♥ KJxxx	7/3 ♥ xx	7/3 ♥ xx
♦ AKQxx	♦ Jxx	♦ Jxxx
♣ Ax	♣ Kxxx	♣ KQx

8·1 + 3 = 11·1 　　　　　　　　8·1 + 3 = 11·1

2♥	3♣	2♥	3♣
3♦	3NT	3♦	4♦
Pass		5♦	Pass

Opener	Responder A	Responder B
♠ AQx	♠ xxxx	♠ Kxxxx
17/7·1 ♥ KJx	7/3 ♥ Qxx	8/3·1 ♥ xx
♦ AQJxxx	♦ xx	♦ Jxx
♣ x	♣ KQxx	♣ Axx

(7·1 + 3 = 10·1) 　　　　　　7·1 + 3·1 = 10·2

2♦	3♣	2♦	2♠
3NT	Pass	3♠	4♠

When Responder A bids 3♣, having failed to bid a four-card major suit, it is very likely that he holds high cards in clubs. An opener with fewer points would sign off in 3♦. Responder B's bid of 2♠ might be made on a four-card suit, so the opener with only three spades gives a single raise. With four, he would go directly to game.

CHAPTER SEVEN:
OPENING BIDS OF TWO CLUBS

This artificial bid is used for both suited and non-suited hands which can make game with very little help from your partner. In the case of balanced hands, the minimum requirement is 23 points as in many other systems. The negative response is 2♦. With 23 or 24 points, the opener rebids 2NT and this can be passed if partner is valueless. Any other sequence of bids after a 2♣ opener is forcing to game. With a non-suited hand of 25 or more points, the opener bids 3NT over the 2♦ response.

After the 2♣ - 2♦ - 2NT sequence, the responder should bid in a manner similar to his response to an opening 2NT bid, but allowing for the extra strength of the opening 2♣.

	♠ AQxx		♠ Jxxx
23/8·1	♥ Ax	2/1·1	♥ xxxx
	♦ KQxx		♦ Jxx
	♣ AKJ		♣ xx

$$8\cdot1 + 1\cdot1 = 9\cdot2$$

2♣		2♦
2NT		3♣
3♠		4♠

The 3♣ bid is a fair gamble, holding four cards in both majors.

With suited hands, the 2♣ opener covers the bids of 2♠, 2♥, and 2♦ in standard systems, as well as 2♣. These hands are so rare that it is a pity to use four bids when one will do. The requirement depends a little on whether the suit is a major or minor, bearing in mind that the bid is forcing to game. The normal minimum is about 8·2 winners. The following qualify for 2♣.

	♠ x		♠ AKxxxx		♠ KQJxxxx		♠ Ax
21/8·2	♥ AKQxxx	19/9	♥ KQJx	17/9	♥ AKxx	22/9·1	♥ KQx
	♦ KQx		♦ AQx		♦ A		♦ AKQxxx
	♣ AKx		♣ -		♣ x		♣ Ax

Responses to 2♣

The negative response of 2♦ shows a lack of one Norman point, i.e., no Ace and no more than one King. With an Ace or two Kings or better, respond in a five-card or longer suit (2♠, 2♥, 3♦, 3♣) or bid 2NT when non-suited. It is usually up to the responder to make the running towards a slam.

	♠ AKxxx		♠ Qxxx
19/9	♥ AKxxx	7/4	♥ Qx
	♦ KQx		♦ xx
	♣ -		♣ Kxxxx

$$9 + 4 = 13$$

2♣	2♦
2♠	3♣
3♥	5♠
6♠	Pass

CHAPTER EIGHT:
PRE-EMPTIVE BIDS

This chapter covers hands with long suits but weak in points. We have already considered bids with long solid minor suits (open 3NT) and strong club suits (open 3♣). There remains consideration of opening bids of 3 or 4 of a major, 3♦, and 4 or 5 of a minor. These are the pure pre-emptive bids of the system. Ely Culbertson, many years ago, said almost the last word on these when he stated his "Law of Two and Three." Do not risk going down more than two tricks vulnerable or three tricks not vulnerable in order to obstruct your opponents. These correspond to a penalty of 500.

Bids of five of a major are special bids, stating that the opener can take every trick except the Ace and King of trumps.

Reverting to the normal pre-emptive bids, the responder should almost invariably allow that his partner has named the trump suit. He should raise, but not above game, if he has four high card tricks not vulnerable or three tricks vulnerable. For example, not vulnerable:

Opener	Responder A	Responder B
♠ x	♠ KJxxx	♠ Axxxx
♥ AQJxxxx	♥ x	♥ K
♦ xxx	♦ Axx	♦ AKxx
♣ xx	♣ Axxx	♣ xxx
3♥	No bid	4♥
(six probable tricks)	(only three possible high card tricks)	(four probable high card tricks)

47

Exceptions may be made when responding to 3♦. When holding some trump support (e.g., Qx) and stops in the other suits, bid 3NT. When holding an independent major suit of sufficient strength, bid 4 of the major. A bid of 3 of a major is asking for support for it, but shows sufficient values for play in 4♦ when that support is lacking. E.g., not vulnerable:

	Opener		Responder
	♠ Qx		♠ KJxxxx
8/5·1	♥ x	15/6·2	♥ Kxx
	♦ KQJxxxx		♦ Ax
	♣ xxx		♣ Ax

$$5·1 + 6·2 = 12$$

| | 3♦ | | 3♠ |
| | 4♠ | | Pass |

With such hands, duplication of values (as in this case in hearts) is probable so that a count of winners may be optimistic. If the responder had bid 3♥, the opener would have rebid 4♦.

Over an opening 3 of a major, the response 4 of the other major shows serious hopes of game in that suit.

CHAPTER NINE:
SUMMARY OF SYSTEM

Hands are divided between those with five-card or longer suit (suited hands) and those without. The latter are initially expected to play in No Trumps and are valued by usual 4,3,2,1 points. The former are initially expected to play in a suit contract and are valued by "winners." High card winners are derived from points (P) by the formula $1/3$ (P-1) and are approximately the same as King values. However, valuation by points is all that is required for No Trumps. Distributional winners are derived from the short suits where card fewer than three are counted, e.g., two for a singleton and one for a doubleton. Both kinds of winners are trick expectations and are added together to give the total winners in a suited hand. The trick expectation of the partnership when there are eight or more trumps is the sum of their individual winners, but when there is no agreement on the trump suit, winners should not be added. A $1/3$ fraction (written as ·1) is a 33 percent chance of a trick, while $2/3$ (expressed as ·2) is a 67 percent chance. 25 points are normally required for a bid of 3NT, 33 for 6NT, and 37 for 7NT. A major suit game should be bid with eight or more trumps and at least 9·2 winners.

The first bid made by a player, other than in support for partner's suit, indicates with a few well-defined exceptions whether or not he has a suited hand. Four-card suits may be shown subsequently.

Opening Bids — No Five-card Suit

1♣ ("weak 1♣")   13 - 15 points
  Also used for 4,4,4,1 distribution and 16 - 22 points
1NT   16 - 19 points
  Subsequently divided weaker 16, 17 and stronger 18, 19 points
2♣   23 or more points

Opening Bids — Suited Hands

1♣   club suit and   13 - 22 points (5 - 8·1 winners)

1♠ 1♥ 1♦   5 - 6·2 winners; below 18 points
Note 1NT for 5,3,3,2 hands with a minor suit and 16 or 17 points

2♠ 2♥ 2♦   7 - 8·1 winners or 18 points

2♣   any suit   8·2 or more winners

Bids of 3 or 4 of a suit and 3NT are pre-emptive based on a long suit.

Responses

The form of subsequent bidding depends on the opening bid. The bids 1♣ and 2♣ are absolutely forcing and require a reply — negative 1♦ or 2♦, respectively, with a weak hand. A response in NT is not used with a poor hand. It is replaced by a minimum bid of clubs when responding to the strong, but not forcing, bids of 2♠ 2♥ 2♦ and 1NT.

Bidding in support of partner's suit is based on a count of winners, assuming he has the minimum shown by his bidding. Such support normally shows that the partnership has at least eight trumps.

 E.g.,
Opening 1♥ (5 winners)   reply 2♥ on 3 winners
           (5 + 3 = 8 tricks expected)
           reply 3♥ on 4 winners
           (5 + 4 = 9 tricks expected)

In the case of non-suit hands three strengths are recognised:

1. Minimum response to a strong opener (1NT 2♠ 2♥ 2♦)6 - 8 points
2. Minimum response to a weak opener (1♠ 1♥ 1♦ 1♣) 9 - 11 points
3. Strong hand expecting game   12+ points

In the case of suited hands, the requirements are approximately:

1. Minimum response to a strong opening bid   2·1 or more winners
2. Minimum response to a weak opening bid   3 or more winners
3. Forcing response to a strong opener and 1♣   5 or more winners
4. Forcing response to a weak opener 1♠ 1♥ 1♦   6 or more winners

In subsequent bidding to repeat one's suit or give minimum support for partner's indicates a relatively weak hand.

Some Considerations Relating to Sequences Following Particular Opening Bids

1. Opening 1♠ 1♥ 1♦. These are limit bids and can be passed with fewer than 3 winners or 9 points.

2. After the 1♣ opener, the positive responses 1NT 1♠ 1♥ are limited and can be passed. The forcing responses are any at the two level. It is assumed that 1♣ means short suits and 13 - 15 points, unless the opener's rebid shows that this is not so.

After the negative 1♦ response, any suit rebid by the opener at the two level shows a strong hand and therefore a club suit, in addition to the bid suit (if not 2♣). 2NT over the 1♦ response shows 4,4,4,1 distribution and 20 - 22 points.

A subsequent club bid by the opener shows at least five clubs. A four-card heart suit is normally bid before spades. A jump rebid in another suit shows a two-suiter with clubs.

3. 2♠, 2♥, and 2♦ are strong but limited, and can be passed with fewer than 2 winners or 6 points. A 3♣ response is artificial, showing a little strength.

4. 1NT opener. This has a 4-point spread. Subsequent bidding differentiates between the weaker and stronger hands. The 2♣ response on 6 - 8 points does not necessarily show a four-card major, but does enable the opener to bid one at the appropriate level according to his points.

How to Describe the System for Opponents

Strong NT   16 - 19 points
Three-way 1♣ with negative 1♦ response:
     1. Weak balanced hand, 13 - 15 points.
     2. Club suit.
     3. 4,4,4,1 distribution, 13 - 22 points.
Limited opening bids of 1♠, 1♥, and 1♦, showing five or more cards.

Intermediate strength bids of 2♠, 2♥, and 2♦.
Forcing 2♣ with negative 2♦.
No weak NT response.
Minimum response in clubs to a strong bid shows 6+ points.
Slam conventions — Blackwood, Cue Bids, 5NT Grand Slam force.

Points to Remember

Opening Bid

23 or more	2♣
20 - 22	2NT
16, 17	1NT including five-card minor
18, 19	1NT higher range
13 - 15	1♣

Responding Bids

15, 16 (4,3,3,3 distribution)	3NT to 1 bid (slam suggestion)
12 - 14 and higher	Game force over 1♠, 1♥, 1♦, and 1♣
9 - 11, 12 - 14	Game force over 1NT
9 - 11	1NT to 1♠, 1♥, 1♦, and 1♣
6 - 8	Response to 1NT, 2♠, 2♥, and 2♦

Winners to Remember

Opening Bid

8·2 or more	2♣
7 - 8·1	2♠, 2♥, 2♦, and strong 1♣
5 - 6·2	1♠, 1♥, 1♦, and 1♣

Responding Bids

6 or more	Jump take-out over 1♠, 1♥, and 1♦
5 or more	Jump take-out over 1NT Two-level response to 1♣
4 - 4·1	Jump suit raise
3 - 3·2	Minimum response to 1♠, 1♥, and 1♦ Positive response to 1♣
2 or more	Minimum response to 2♠, 2♥, and 2♦

PART THREE

CHAPTER TEN:
SOME COMPARISONS OF
SYSTEMS AND CONVENTIONS

The 1NT Controversy

The Acol system has the two limit bids of 1NT with 12 -14 points not vulnerable, and an optional 15 - 17 points vulnerable as a safety measure. Since these limits affect other calls, it requires one to learn, in effect, two different systems. Many people therefore decide to use either the weak or the strong NT throughout.

The weak bid is undoubtedly of value as a barricade, but it runs the risk of a large penalty, especially when vulnerable. It has some protection because of the unlimited nature of a responding pass. This can be made with up to 10 points, so the partnership total could be from 12 - 24 points, the average being 18 — less than half the total.

As shown in the Appendix, it is always better to double 1NT for penalty than to bid NT yourself at equal vulnerability, and especially when non-vulnerable against vulnerable opponents.

The Cleveland Club uses only a strong NT — stronger than the Acol strong NT — so we only have to consider the safety of the weak 1♣ opener. The following factors apply:

i)   The minimum is 13 rather than 12 points.

ii)   If partner is weak, we usually end in 1♠, 1♥, or even 1♦, where a double would be for take-out.

iii) If we have to bid 1NT over the negative 1♦ response, we are showing a club suit which gives a possible safe escape.

iv)   Partner responding 1♦ could have up to 8 points, so that we might have 23 points between us.

In fifty years of using this convention, I have never been successfully doubled in 1NT after opening 1♣.

Another disadvantage of the modern weak Acol NT is that it makes it impossible to find a suit fit when, as is likely, the responder cannot reply, having less than 11 points, or is unsuitable for a weak suit take-out. Some hands with scattered strength, passed with a five-card suit, might play better in the suit. However, with weaker balanced hands there is a good chance of a 4-4 fit, which cannot be found in Acol. For example, the following are common types of hands:

Opener	Responder	Acol Bidding		Cleveland Bidding	
♠ AKxx	♠ xx				
13/5 ♥ AQxx	4/2 ♥ xxxx	1NT	Pass	1♣	1♦
♦ xxx	♦ QJxx			1♥	Pass
♣ xx	♣ Jxx				

There is no escape from a double of 1NT, while 1♥ is a much safer contract.

Problems with Unlimited Bids of One of a Suit

While it is always possible to produce hands which give problems to any system, I don't believe the following examples are unfair. 5,3,3,2 distribution is common. Let us suppose we have as responder:

♠ xx   ♥ xxx   ♦ KJx   ♣ Kxxxx   7/3

In Acol, we will reply 1NT to partner's opening 1♠, 1♥, or 1♦, but in the Cleveland Club we will pass 1♠ and raise 1♥ or 1♦ to 2.

Opener	Responder	Standard Bidding		Cleveland Bidding	
♠ AKJxx	♠ xx				
12/4·2 ♥ Kxx	7/3 ♥ xxx	1♠	1NT	1♠	Pass
♦ xx	♦ KJx	Pass			
♣ Jxx	♣ Kxxxx				

With hands like these, the standard players will be trying to make seven tricks in NT with less than half the points.

Opener	Responder	Standard Bidding		Cleveland Bidding	
♠ Kxx	♠ xx				
13/5 ♥ AQxxx	7/3 ♥ xxx	1♥	1NT	1♥	2♥
♦ Axx	♦ KJx	Pass		Pass	
♣ xx	♣ Kxxxx				

2♥ is a better prospect than 1NT, especially after a spade lead, and is a better barricade.

Opener	Responder	Standard Bidding		Cleveland Bidding	
♠ AKxxx	♠ xx				
19/7 ♥ Kxx	7/3 ♥ xxx	1♠	1NT	2♠	3♣
♦ Ax	♦ KJx	3NT	Pass	3NT	Pass
♣ AJx	♣ Kxxxx				

Both pairs reach 3NT, but in the Cleveland Club system the strong hand is the declarer. An opening lead of the Queen of hearts could wreck the standard pair, but leaves the Cleveland pair with a good prospect.

In each of the three examples, the weaker hand becomes the declarer in standard, but in Cleveland the stronger hand becomes the declarer.

The problems arising from not knowing whether the opener has a four-card or longer suit were mentioned in the introduction. The advantages of having the opening bids 1♠, 1♥, and 1♦ limited and restricted to suited hands are clear.

Transfer Bids

There has been a vogue for the use of transfer bids in response to a strong 1NT opener, to allow the strong hand to be the declarer in partner's suit. This extra artificial bid seems to be an undesirable complication for the following reasons:

1. The lead up to the strong hand is not as important in a suit contract as in NT.
2. The main trump suit is displayed in dummy in the transfer sequence.
3. A natural bid of 2♦ by the responder is prevented. Some hands should play in diamonds.
4. The opener's rebid after the transfer is purely automatic and therefore, in a sense, wasted.
5. An opportunity is given to the opponents to request a damaging lead, as in the following hand from a team of four match.

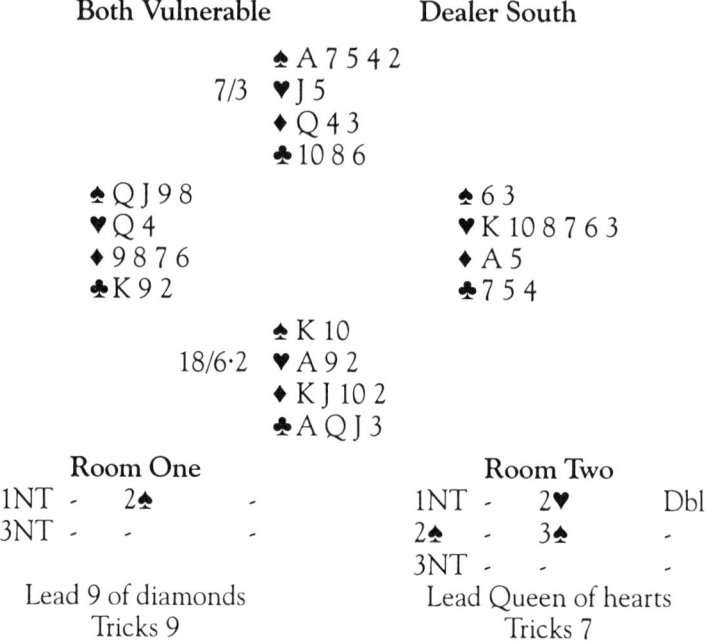

Both Vulnerable   Dealer South

                    ♠ A 7 5 4 2
          7/3   ♥ J 5
                    ♦ Q 4 3
                    ♣ 10 8 6

♠ Q J 9 8   ♠ 6 3
♥ Q 4   ♥ K 10 8 7 6 3
♦ 9 8 7 6   ♦ A 5
♣ K 9 2   ♣ 7 5 4

                    ♠ K 10
          18/6·2   ♥ A 9 2
                    ♦ K J 10 2
                    ♣ A Q J 3

Room One				Room Two		
1NT	-	2♠	-	1NT	-	2♥	Dbl
3NT	-	-	-	2♠	-	3♠	-
				3NT	-	-	-

Lead 9 of diamonds   Lead Queen of hearts
Tricks 9   Tricks 7

Using the Opponent's Suit

An immediate bid of the opponent's opening suit is commonly used to show a powerful hand with not more than one card in the suit named. It is stronger than an informatory double, and some players use it to show a two-suiter. A bid of the opponent's suit after we have agreed trumps is used as a cue bid showing first round control. The purpose of this section is to describe the use of the opponent's suit when we have a good hand with a difficult bid. This is often used by standard players, but is of especial value in the Cleveland Club after a 1NT or 1♣ opener. For example, partner's opening 1NT is over-called by 2♦. We hold:

  ♠ Axxx   ♥ Axxx   ♦ xx   ♣ Qxx   10/4

With no intervening bid, we would force with 2NT and hope to play in 4 of a major. After the intervening bid, 2NT implies a stop in diamonds. We resolve this dilemma by bidding 3♦. Some players use a "negative double" in this situation. This works well, but prevents the use of a business double which can be more fun; for example, with:

  ♠ xx   ♥ xxx   ♦ KJ9x   ♣ Axxx   8·3/1

The bid of the opponent's suit is also of value in response to an informatory double or 1NT overcall. For example, your left-hand opponent opens 1♥, doubled by partner. You hold:

♠ Jxxx   ♥ xx   ♦ AQx   ♣ Kxxx   10/4

1♠ would be much too weak a bid, and 2♠ rather misleading. 2♥ shows the strength of the hand, and the spades can be shown later in support of partner.

PART FOUR

CHAPTER ELEVEN:
BIDDING IN COMPETITIVE SITUATIONS

Whichever system is chosen for bidding when the opponents do not take part, there is a measure of agreement on how to bid when the opponents have opened.

Combatting Pre-emptive Bids

The first thing is to recognise is that the pre-emptive bidder has succeeded in his aim of denying our side three or four rounds of bidding. This means that we are in more of a gambling situation than when we open the bidding. It is necessary to consider vulnerability and use judgment.

Various methods have been used to limit the damage inflicted by the pre-empt. We recommend the simplest — optional doubles of 3 bids to invite partner to bid his best suit, with other bids including 3NT natural. For example, over 3♥:

	♠ AQJxxx		♠ AQxx		♠ Kxx
13/6	♥ x	14/6·1	♥ x	19/7	♥ AQx
	♦ Kxx		♦ Axxx		♦ KQJxx
	♣ Kxx		♣ Axxx		♣ Ax
	Bid 3♠		Double		Bid 3NT

63

Response to Optional Double of a Pre-empt

Partner with values in the opponent's suit may convert the double into a business double by passing, but will usually prefer to select a suit. In this case, preference should be given to a major suit. For example, partner has doubled 3♥:

♠ Kxxx	♠ Axxxx	♠ Kxx	♠ Jxx
6/2·2 ♥ xxx	9/3·2 ♥ xx	9/2·2 ♥ QJxx	11 ♥ AK
♦ Kxxx	♦ KJx	♦ xxx	♦ Qxxx
♣ xx	♣ Jxx	♣ Kxx	♣ Jxxx
Reply 3♠	Reply 4♠	Pass	Reply 3NT

When the pre-empt is at the four level, it is more difficult to find our best contract. The optional double is more often converted to business unless the responder has a long suit.

Overcalls

When the opponents open the bidding, we have a problem with non-suited hands because we can easily be doubled if we bid a four-card suit.

With suited hands, we may have a variety of motives in bidding besides proposing a successful contract — namely, to suggest a lead or prepare for a sacrifice. Culbertson's "Law of Two and Three," mentioned in Chapter Eight, which limits losses to 500 if doubled, is a good guide. Besides vulnerability, we have to consider our position at the table relative to the bidding opponent.

A simple suit overcall is a limit bid, and it is necessary to indicate a good hand by a jump bid or an informatory double. For example, when not vulnerable, after 1♥ from the right-hand opponent, bid as shown:

♠ KQxxx	♠ QJxx	♠ AKQxx	♠ Axxx
8/4·1 ♥ xx	8/4·1 ♥ xx	16/7 ♥ x	14/6·1 ♥ x
♦ QJxx	♦ KQxxx	♦ AQJx	♦ AQxxx
♣ xx	♣ xx	♣ xxx	♣ Axx
Bid 1♠	Pass	Bid 2♠	Double
	2♦ is too risky		

The first example shows that the value for a simple overcall can be lower than for an opening bid.

After two passes, we can reopen the bidding with a slightly weaker hand. This is considered more fully on the following page.

64

Overcalls in Second and Fourth Positions

When the player on our right has made a bid but his partner has yet to speak, we may find ourselves between the hammer and the anvil — a strong hand on each side. A double of our suit overcall by the left-hand opponent is, of course, a business double. This shows that we need a suit of at least five cards to bid it. Over 1♥ it could be disastrous to bid 1♠ on:

♠ KJxx	♥ xxx	♦ AQx	♣ Kxx	13/4

if the left-hand opponent has something like:

♠ AQxx	♥ x	♦ Kxx	♣ Jxxxx	10/5

Our hand qualifies for an opening bid, but its values are defensive. The opponents are unlikely to be able to make game.

With non-suit hands we should therefore pass, unless strong enough to bid 1NT (16 points) or make an informatory double (at least 5·1 winners). Again, over a 1♥ bid on our right hand, bid as shown:

♠ xxxx	♠ Kxxx	♠ Kxxx	♠ Qxx
11/5·1 ♥ x	15/5·2 ♥ xx	17 ♥ AQx	12/4·2 ♥ xx
♦ AQxx	♦ AKx	♦ Kxx	♦ AJxx
♣ AJxx	♣ AJxx	♣ AJx	♣ KQxx
Double	Double	1NT	Pass

As a consequence of this, the player in the fourth position, whose pass would close the auction, should consider the possibility that his partner might have passed on, for example, a hand suitable for a weak 1♣ opener. The opponents should not have passed up an opportunity for a game contract, so we should have nothing to lose if they continue the bidding. The requirement for an informatory double and for a suit bid can therefore be reduced in fourth position. After 1♥ and two passes, bid as shown:

♠ Kxx	♠ Qxxx	♠ AJxxx
11/4·1 ♥ xx	9/4·2 ♥ x	10/4 ♥ xx
♦ QJxx	♦ Kxxx	♦ Qxx
♣ AJxx	♣ Axxx	♣ Kxx
Double	Double	1♠

Responding to Overcalls

Since a simple suit overcall is limited, we must be careful in replying. It is usually better to raise partner's suit rather than introduce your own. This is partly for safety reasons, but it is also better tactics, since it may be the only opportunity to show that we agree on a suit. Your partner will realise that his suit is unlikely to take many tricks in defence if you support it. If you do not, you may be short in it and could possibly get a ruff. Of course, these considerations should not stop you from mentioning a good major suit if partner has bid a minor. In the examples, your partner has bid 1♥ over 1♦ at equal vulnerability:

♠ KQx	♠ AQJxx	♠ AQJxxx
9/3·2 ♥ xxx	8/3·1 ♥ xxx	8/4·1 ♥ xx
♦ xx	♦ xx	♦ xx
♣ Axxxx	♣ Jxx	♣ Jxx
Support hearts	Support hearts	Bid spades

On the other hand, if our partner makes a jump overcall and we have some strength, our main consideration is to find the best game contract. Again, partner's major suit should be supported if we have three cards in it.

The response to an informatory double is forced unless we have length in the opponent's suit and decide to convert to a business double by passing. A simple suit bid, therefore, makes no promise of strength. If we have a hand which could respond to a limited opening bid, we must jump the bidding. In the examples, partner has doubled 1♥:

♠ xxxx	♠ Jxxxx	♠ x	♠ KQJxxx
♥ xx	9/3·2 ♥ xx	3/2·2 ♥ QJxxxx	9/4·2 ♥ x
♦ xxxx	♦ Axx	♦ xxx	♦ Qxx
♣ xxx	♣ KJx	♣ xxx	♣ Jxx
Bid 1♠	Bid 2♠	Pass	Bid 4♠

Business and Optional Doubles

Light business doubles can be made of contracts scoring 40 points or less, since they do not give game if the contract succeeds. However, a doubler of a 60 - 90 point contract should normally be certain that the contract will fail. Doubles of game contracts, often called free doubles, may not be so, especially if there is a redouble.

Doubles of suit contracts can come to grief in the face of an abnormal trump holding or distribution. For safety, the doubler should have a fair holding of trumps. Doubles of NT are more likely to be successful on the basis of points.

We have seen an example of an optional double in dealing with a pre-emptive bid. Optional doubles are also recommended for competing with 1NT, whether made immediately as:

	1♥	Pass	1NT	Double
and	1NT	Double		

or after two passes as

	1♥	Pass	1NT	Pass
	Pass	Double		
and	1NT	Pass	Pass	Double

Whether the opening NT bid is weak or strong, we need to be stronger in order to compete on a profitable basis. That is, we need 18 points to challenge a strong NT and 15 points to challenge the weak NT. About the same number of points (15) should be held when challenging the NT response to an unlimited suit opener — slightly more for the immediate double and slightly less for the reopening double.

This advice is based on the calculations in the appendix, which show that it is better to double 1NT than to bid NT ourselves.

There is, of course, some risk in the double, and this is the reason for making it optional. A partner weak in points but with a long suit can rescue into the suit. For example, partner has doubled a weak NT and it has been left by the opener's partner:

	♠ xx		♠ Kxxx		♠ Axx		♠ Axxxxx
1/2	♥ xx	9	♥ Qxx	10/4	♥ xx	7/4	♥ x
	♦ Jxxxxx		♦ Jxxx		♦ KQJxx		♦ Kxx
	♣ xxx		♣ Kx		♣ xxx		♣ xxx
	Bid 2♦		Penalty Pass		Penalty Pass		Bid 3♠

In the last example, there is a good prospect of game in spades, while the 1NT may not go down much. This decision is, of course, affected by relative vulnerability.

Competing When Your Partner Has Opened

In this system, all opening bids (except occasionally 1♣) are limited, and this makes it comparatively easy to respond over an intervening bid. All the artificial responses, such as 3♣ to a strong two bid, are abandoned, and bids are natural.

If we have a number of cards in partner's suit, it becomes more important to put up a barricade by giving the maximum suit raise. This may be especially important after an informatory double. On the other hand, if we are short in partner's suit, our defensive values are enhanced and we should look for an opportunity to double. For example, partner's 1♠ opener has been overcalled by 2♣:

7/4
♠ Jxxx
♥ x
♦ Axxxx
♣ Qxx

11/5·1
♠ x
♥ Kxxx
♦ Axxx
♣ KJxx

Bid 4♠. The opponents may have a heart fit.

Double for penalty — warns partner about lack of fit for spades.

When our partner's opening suit bid has been doubled, we show a good hand by redoubling. This puts pressure on the opponents, especially if the bid was in a major. The opener should normally pass to hear more about the redoubler's hand, but can show a weak long-suited hand by rebidding 2.

APPENDIX:
CALCULATIONS AND
STATISTICS

A. Calculations

Values Required to Bid Game: Does Vulnerability Matter?

The rubber bonus is 500 for a three-game rubber and 700 for a two-game rubber. Since it may be harder to get the second game when opponents are not vulnerable and can afford to take risks to obstruct, the second game is conventionally assumed to be worth 400 points and the first game 300. It follows that a vulnerable game is worth either 400 or 500 points — average 450. Obviously, an equalising second game is also worth 300 points, i.e., non-vulnerable games are worth 300.

If a non-vulnerable part score is worth an additional 50, a vulnerable one should be worth 75 points. Going down one costs 50 or 100 points non-vulnerable (average 75), and 100 or 200 points vulnerable (average 150), depending on whether there is a double. The value of a near game part score is 70, 80, or 90 (average 80) below the line. Using these figures, we can construct the following profit/loss tables.

Not Vulnerable Scores

Game is Bid		Game is Not Bid	
play fails	play succeeds	play fails	play succeeds
-75	400+	80 + 50 = 130	150+

Bidding game therefore leads to a loss of 205 if it fails and a gain of 250 points if it succeeds.

Vulnerable Scores (average game bonus 450)

Game is Bid		Game is Not Bid	
play fails	play succeeds	play fails	play succeeds
-150	550+	80 + 75 = 155	175+

Bidding game therefore leads to a loss of 305 if it fails and a gain of 375 if it succeeds.

It follows that in both cases, game should be bid if there is almost a 50 percent chance of making it. Vulnerability does not affect the odds — it only raises the stakes.

Points Needed for No Trump Game

When there are trumps, the trick expectation is simply the sum of individual winners. This assumes that the loss caused by duplication of values is balanced by the "thirteenth trick" when we have control by having eight trumps. We bid a major suit game when our combined winners are $9\cdot2$ ($9^2/_3$).

In No Trumps, there is no need to make an allowance for duplication of values. On the other hand, control is less certain when there are no trumps. We assume that we make the thirteenth trick in three cases out of four — giving an allowance of 3/4 trick. The total trick expectation from high cards is:

$$\frac{P1 - 1}{3} \quad + \quad \frac{P2 - 1}{3} \quad \text{i.e.,} \quad \frac{P1 + P2 - 2}{3}$$

Where P1 and P2 are the points in two partnership hands. We wish to bid 3NT if we have nearly a 50 percent chance of getting nine tricks. Using arithmetical notation:

$$\frac{P1 + P2 - 2}{3} \quad + \quad 0\cdot75 \quad = \quad 8\cdot5$$

from which $P1 + P2 = 25$

This figure is generally accepted and leads to the need to bid a 13-point hand, but not a 12-point hand, to be sure of not missing a 3NT game.

Slam Bidding and Vulnerability

We can construct similar profit/loss tables for slams, but we do not need to allow for being doubled.

Small Slam Not Vulnerable

Slam Bid		Slam Not Bid	
11 tricks made	12 tricks made	11 tricks made	12 tricks made
-50	800 + 160	300 + 130	300 + 160

Loss on bidding slam but failing — 480
Gain on bidding slam and making — 500

Small Slam Vulnerable

Slam Bid		Slam Not Bid	
11 tricks made	12 tricks made	11 tricks made	12 tricks made
-100	1200 + 160	450 + 130	450 + 160

Loss on bidding slam but failing — 680
Gain on bidding slam and making — 750

Whether vulnerable or not, we should bid on a 50 percent chance of success.

Grand Slam Not Vulnerable

Grand Slam Bid		Only Small Slam Bid	
12 tricks made	13 tricks made	12 tricks made	13 tricks made
-50	1300 + 190	800 + 160	800 + 190

Loss on bidding grand slam but failing — 1010
Gain on bidding grand slam and making — 500

Grand Slam Vulnerable

Grand Slam Bid		Only Small Slam Bid	
12 tricks made	13 tricks made	12 tricks made	13 tricks made
-100	1950 + 190	1200 + 160	1200 + 190

Loss on bidding grand slam but failing — 1460
Gain on bidding grand slam and making — 750

Whether vulnerable or not, we should not bid the grand slam unless we have 2 chances in 3 (67%) of making it.

Double of 1NT

It always pays to double 1NT rather than bid NT ourselves, unless we can make a vulnerable game and opponents are not vulnerable. The following tables show the gains from doubling.

Neither Vulnerable

Our tricks	Our bid	Score	Score by doubling 1NT	Gain
7	2NT	-50	100	150
8	2NT	120	300	180
9	3NT	400	500	100

Both Vulnerable

Our tricks	Our bid	Score	Score by doubling 1NT	Gain
7	2NT	-100	200	300
8	2NT	145	500	355
9	3NT	600	800	200

Opponents Vulnerable

Our tricks	Our bid	Score	Score by doubling 1NT	Gain
7	2NT	-50	200	250
8	2NT	120	500	380
9	3NT	400	800	400

We Are Vulnerable

Our tricks	Our bid	Score	Score by doubling 1NT	Gain
7	2NT	-100	100	200
8	2NT	145	300	155
9	3NT	600	500	-100

Even in the last case it is better to double, since there is no risk.

B. Statistics

Frequency of Card Distributions

Owing to imperfect shuffling, in practice the distribution of hand shapes is different from the theoretical figures. The following percentages show a comparison between a 500 sample and the theoretical figures.

Non-suited Hands			Suited Hands		
Theoretical percentage	Sample percentage			Theoretical percentage	Sample percentage
		5,3,3,2		16	17
4,3,3,3 11	19	5,4,3,1		13	11
4,4,3,2 22	26	5,4,2,2		11	9
4,4,4,1 3	3	all 6 & 2 5 cards		20	13
		all others		5	3
36	48			65	53

When holding a five-card suit, the chances of your partner's having at least three cards are:

theoretical	54·5 percent	either 3 or 4 cards are	48 percent
practical (approx.)	57·5 percent	either 3 or 4 cards are	52 percent

When holding a four-card suit, the chances of your partner's having at least four cards are:

theoretical	33·7 percent	just 4 cards are	22 percent
practical (approx.)	36 percent	just 4 cards are	25 percent

A partner with five or more cards would bid the suit anyway.

These figures show the fundamental difference between the four-card and longer suits.

When the combined holding is eight cards, the chances of finding an opponent with four or more cards are:

theoretical	32 percent
practical (approx.)	28 percent

When the combined holding is seven cards, the chances of finding an opponent with four or more cards are:

theoretical	64·5 percent
practical (approx.)	60 percent

Culbertson's Rule of Symmetrical Tendencies

This can be roughly restated as "Singletons occur in pairs." That is, if you can see one singleton, suspect another in your long suit.

Distribution of Points

Bid on non-suited hands	Points	Approximate percentage
Pass	0 - 12	73
1♣	13 - 15	16
1NT	16 - 19	8·5
2NT	20 - 22	2
2♣	above 22	0·4

Only about 8 percent of the non-suited hands which qualify for a bid could open at the two level.

Comparison of Two Different Point Counts

There was a time when the following point count was in fairly common use:

Ace	7	
King	5	16 per suit
Queen	3	64 total
Jack	1	

To convert from the 4321 count, multiply by 1·6. The corresponding figure to 33 for a small slam is therefore 53. While the 33 allows the opponents an Ace and King, the 53 does not.

The corresponding figure to 25 for 3NT is 40. The minimum for a 1♣ bid then becomes 20, and the table of frequencies is:

Bid on non-suited hands	Points	Frequency percentage
Pass	0 - 19	69·8
1♣	20 - 25	20·8
1NT	26 - 31	7·6
2NT	32 - 35	1·4
2♣	36 and up	0·4

This means that, using the 7531 count, one can open about 3 percent more non-suited hands (a 10 percent increase on biddable hands), which is surely a significant advantage.

Of course, one can open even more hands by having a 12-point minimum on the 4321 count, but this requires partner to have a stronger hand for game. There is also an increased hazard when bidding 1NT on 12 points. My Acol friends may wish to consider the 7531 count where the appropriate range for 1NT would be even more precise at 20 - 23 points.